# WALTZING MATILDA

## in French & Spanish

My third book of memories

VALERIE BARNES

Published in Australia by Sid Harta Books & Print Pty Ltd,
ABN: 34632585293
23 Stirling Crescent, Glen Waverley, Victoria 3150  Australia
Telephone: +61 3 9560 9920, Facsimile: +61 3 9545 1742
E-mail: author@sidharta.com.au

First published in Australia 2021
This edition published 2021
Copyright © Valerie Barnes 2021
Cover design, typesetting: WorkingType (www.workingtype.com.au)
Cover photo by Jean-Louis Sagliocco
Cover designed by Luke Harris

The right of Valerie Barnes to be identified as the
Author of the Work has been asserted in accordance with the
Copyright, Designs and Patents Act 1988.

All rights reserved. No part of this publication may be reproduced, stored in a retrieval system, or transmitted, in any form or by any means without the prior written permission of the publisher, nor be otherwise circulated in any form of binding or cover other than that in which it is published and without a similar condition being imposed on the subsequent purchaser.

Barnes, Valerie
*Waltzing Matilda in French and Spanish: My Third Book of Memories*
ISBN: 978-1-925707-58-8
pp238

## About the Author

Born in London, Valerie Taylor Bouladon Barnes moved to Geneva to work for United Nations at the age of 21, soon after the end of WWII when the organisation was young and full of hope, everyone believing that if they based everything on compromise, there would be no more war.

She became a simultaneous interpreter in English, French and Spanish and a translator in Russian. Having fallen in love with an Australian conference delegate, she came to live in Australia in 1979, where she worked for Prime Ministers Bob Hawke and Paul Keating at both the old and new parliament houses. She danced with Bob Hawke in a restaurant in Geneva and was captivated by his aftershave and hairstyle and enjoyed the challenge of translating Paul Keating's vocabulary into French and Spanish.

She has worked and travelled in 98 countries and had many adventures mostly before tourism took over the world. She has many stories to tell: this is her third book of memories and at 94 she is still writing!

*This book is not fiction; it is entirely true except for a few names, which have been changed to protect privacy. The chronology, however, cannot be guaranteed.*

# PREFACE

'Thank you for electing me to this high-ranking post. It is a great honour. I shall do my best to live up to your expectations. I don't intend to make a long speech. I shall, instead, ask the interpreter to please sing *Waltzing Matilda* in French and Spanish.'

The band struck up. All eyes were on me …

# PROLOGUE

We met in Geneva in the early 1970s during an international telecommunications conference, part of the United Nations. He was the leader of the Australian delegation, chairing the meeting from behind a microphone on the podium, one hand pressing an earphone closer to his ear for fear of missing a word. I was an interpreter high up under the ceiling in one of the glass interpretation booths facing him, leaning forward as I concentrated on searching for the rationale behind the speaker's words. Between us, with their backs to me, sat 1000 or so ear-phoned delegates from the 127 member-countries in neat rows of tables with microphones placed at regular intervals.

There were two of us in each interpretation booth; in turn we were on air for half an hour. I was in the English booth, so every other half hour it was my voice he heard in his headphones whenever anyone in the auditorium spoke in French, Spanish or Russian.

The Chairman's voice had a buttery warmth that appealed

to me, and all through that long meeting I made mine sound as sexy as I could. In my line of work, voices are of great importance: I need to comprehend immediately what is being said, so I particularly appreciate qualities like clarity and calmness as well as a pleasant, well-modulated tone. From so high up I sometimes cannot see the faces down below very clearly, so their voices are my lifeline. To amuse myself during long, boring speeches while interpreting what they were saying I tried, on a different level of my brain, to imagine their personality, lifestyle, what their wives looked like, how many children they had and whether they could cook or play the piano. This buttery voice sounded particularly gentle and kind.

I have always enjoyed interpreting, nevertheless, I am always thankful when the chairman announces a break and I can race off to join the queue for a quick cup of coffee. As strong as possible — a *ristretto*. Like most simultaneous interpreters, I cannot work without coffee. Just as cars need petrol, so we need coffee. We have to keep our brains alert and ready to tackle the unexpected — we never know what we are going to say next — half-way through a sentence, its ending may take us by surprise. Now that I am retired, whatever I may be doing, I have to have had my mid-morning coffee otherwise start to fade and shrivel and turn into a prune.

On the morning I was telling you about, during just such a much-needed coffee break, a delegate came across to ask me rather hesitantly, if I knew that I had a look-alike in town.'

'I saw someone very much like you on stage last night in a Gilbert and Sullivan production. I went to see *Ruddigore* at the Grand Theatre.'

I immediately recognised his quiet buttery voice as that of the committee chairman for whom I had been trying to sound sexy, so for once I didn't mind being interrupted during my sacred morning coffee. He introduced himself as Peter.

I was struck by the intense blue of his eyes and their sparkle, his boyish look and his handsome tan. It was only when reflecting on our conversation later that I realised his tan was because he had just come from an Australian summer to our Geneva winter.

'She was very much like you to look at. Taller and slimmer, perhaps, but there was a definite resemblance,' he continued.

Amused, I let him waffle on for a while before finally admitting: 'Well, actually, it was me. I was in *Ruddigore* last night.'

He looked confused, which I found endearing, so I explained:

'I'm a member of the UN Gilbert and Sullivan Operatic Society.'

We chatted over our coffee.

'Singing is important to me,' I explained. 'Especially becoming a seventeen-year-old maiden twice a week — though sometimes I would prefer to be Katisha in *The Mikado* so I could rant and rave instead of always being sweet and demure.'

I refrained from telling him how lonely my life had become since my divorce, or that I enjoyed rehearsals as much for the company as for the music. We talked until the meeting reconvened and I had to hurry back to my high perch, more determined than ever to make my voice sound as captivating as possible.

In the conference cafeteria later that week Peter asked if he could join me at lunch one day when I was sitting alone at a big table. As his colleagues wandered past carrying their trays of food, one by one they saw him and asked if they could join us too, and soon I was surrounded by Australians all wanting to know how simultaneous interpretation worked. That was the start of our Australian group. I sensed how much they missed home and family life, particularly in those days when most telecommunication conferences lasted six weeks, some even longer, and they were all staying in boring hotels in a town where everyone spoke French. French was the language spoken in all Geneva restaurants and cafés, all films and plays shown in the cinemas and theatres were in French, which made life difficult for monolingual Australians with nowhere to go in the evenings.

Our Gilbert and Sullivan productions were in English, so at last the Australian, UK, American and other English-speaking delegates had something they could understand.

Women conference delegates were extremely rare then; I believe all-male cocktail parties began to verge on the boring after a while.

One day when fate arranged for us to be alone together for a few moments, Peter asked quietly: 'If I invited you out to lunch, would you accept?'

'I might,' I replied as I walked away, smiling.

From that day on, each morning when I rushed to consult the noticeboard in the interpreters' room to see what my assignments were for the day, I secretly hoped the chairman of my meeting would be Peter of The Buttery Voice who made maritime distress signals sound almost interesting. Not to mention single and double sidebands, sidelobes and tropospheric scatter. Sometimes I was lucky.

Around midnight on the last day of the conference the Final Acts were signed *in extremis*, as usual, by the leaders of the delegations. It was at that moment that it suddenly struck us all, tired as we were, that this was the end of the conference. All the hard work was over. The bonds of friendship that had been created were about to be severed. Wearily removing my headphones, I threw all my now obsolete documents into the wastepaper basket and picked up my handbag ready to leave. I would have liked a chance to bid Peter farewell and bon voyage before he left but looking down into the hall I saw the delegates milling about saying their goodbyes, exchanging business cards and shaking hands, and I realised it was not my place to go into the meeting room to say goodbye to anyone.

But just as I was leaving the building, I heard footsteps behind me.

'How about that lunch we talked about?' the

hoped-for buttery voice asked. 'Tomorrow? I don't leave till late afternoon. Say, *Perle du Lac* at 12.30?'

'Perle du Lac it is,' I replied, heading off towards the carpark, trying not to look too elated.

The next day was sunny and the birds were tweeting in the trees as I got out of my car and walked through the park to the *Perle du Lac* restaurant. We had a delightful lunch. I remember it still in every detail, forty-three years later. Afterwards he accompanied me back to my car; I held out my hand to shake his and thank him for the Swiss-style lunch, but to my surprise he put his hands firmly on my shoulders and kissed me full on the lips. Then he turned and walked away.

Stunned, I got into my car and sat quietly for a few minutes to regain my composure. It was a long time since I had been kissed on the lips. In Geneva, you kissed people on the cheek, even husbands and wives. Kissing on the lips was something very personal that rarely happened outside the bedroom, or at least in the dark. I had no idea how to interpret what had just happened. I'd never met an Australian before: Perhaps it was just an Australian custom?

I sat in the same booth the following week at yet another conference, but on quite a different subject. I was at the World Health Organisation and I was talking about Sexual Abnormalities in the Newborn Child — but my mind kept returning to that kiss.

We met at various conferences in different parts of the world from time to time after that and communicated by aerogram in between. They were sheets of flimsy paper that folded and sealed to form their own pale blue envelopes. Soon we were exchanging one of these every day, then later sometimes two. We told each other everything that had happened and how desperately we missed one another. Sometimes, instead of aerograms I received fat envelopes containing wads of handwritten lightweight almost see-through sheets of notepaper covered in spidery writing from Singapore, Bangkok or Jakarta.

When Peter's long-service leave was due he bought a one-way air ticket to London where he purchased a 22-ft yacht called the *Solent Dove* and, after working on it for several months during which time I visited him whenever I could, he sailed it back to Australia single-handed. This took him a little more than eighteen months, and in between conferences I was able to visit him on five occasions — each time spending several weeks on board.

But as he approached Tahiti, he received the shattering news that his daughter had died while hitch-hiking in Sri Lanka. In his grief he met his son and ex-wife — she had become very frail — and decided he had to go back to Melbourne to look after her.

PART I

# Geneva

I travelled a lot in India in those days and greatly admired their philosophy: However poor people were always ready to share what they had. It seemed to me that the poorer people were, the more generous, and the more they accepted their fate — they simply made the best of what little they had; they seemed content and even happy. They smiled at me knowingly and said: 'Count your blessings. Be content with what you have. It is pointless to yearn for what is beyond your reach.'

I must have absorbed this philosophy, because I accepted without complaint the fact that Peter had returned to live in Melbourne with his wife from whom he had been estranged for several years.

'I have a lot to be grateful for,' I told myself. 'I live in a beautiful country, I have three healthy, intelligent children and a stimulating, exciting career, which enables me to earn enough to pay for all our needs. I can devote all the love I would have given to a man to my three children.'

As I sipped lemon tea under the lilac tree in the garden, the blue *Lac Léman* lay at the foot of the hill and behind it in the distance the sparkling snow-covered Mont Blanc began to turn a crisp pink in the late afternoon sun.

Peter's letters arrived regularly, almost every day, in the green wooden letterbox tucked into the laurel hedge by the front gate. Some were long, others very long; the wad of flimsy airmail paper with spidery writing on both sides was difficult to read. Some were written in blue or black, others even in red. I began to live for the letters and would sometimes drive home at high speed after a hasty lunch in the conference cafeteria to see if there was anything in the letterbox, before rushing back just in time for the start of the afternoon meeting. The trip took exactly seven minutes each way, provided I managed to maintain a regular speed of 140 km/h along the autoroute in my beloved turquoise Fiat 600.

His first letters complained how uncomfortable shoes were after two years' sailing mostly barefoot: His feet were in prison, he said. Wearing a shirt and tie also seemed quite unnecessary as well as unpleasant and unhealthy. Worst of all was being shut up in an office eight hours a day, unable to see the sky, unable to know whether or not the sun was shining outside. How could people live cut off from nature; shut up inside walled boxes for most of their waking hours?

'My yacht needs me just as I need her. She is deteriorating day by day and her upkeep — even just to keep her bottom free of barnacles — is impossible to arrange. She needs someone to warm her from the inside, to open up her soul to the elements, to make her move and live. We are both in prison. She is in a lake in Pambula without a sea horizon and I'm here in an office under artificial light with the only view from my desk being a glass partition 6 ft away.'

Sunrises and sunsets had been his main points of reference — for one hundred and four weeks he had never missed one.

'How has it happened that mankind has developed such an unnatural, sunset-and sunrise-deprived way of life?' he wrote.

Before parting in Rarotonga Airport we had agreed that we would have a holiday together as soon as he had accumulated enough days' leave. It would take some time before he was entitled to two weeks but the thought of being together again raised our spirits. Peter chose a Greek island for our first holiday together, and I suggested Skiathos because that was one I hadn't yet visited.

In the meantime, I had promised Cassie a trip to England that summer — just the two of us, to make up for having been away so often on overseas conferences. If we left Geneva early in the morning in my trusty turquoise Fiat, we could get to London by late the same evening. We had our favourite stopping places in France for morning coffee and lunch, and I usually made a *détour* in order to drive through Chartres because I wanted Cassie to see the cathedral which, for me, was the most beautiful in the world. You are driving along a straight flat road and suddenly this Gothic cathedral rises up to your right, out of nowhere. Standing, looking at its magnificent twelfth and thirteenth century blue stained-glass windows, we were transported into a different spiritual realm. Although the cathedral is the product of what today we would call an illiterate society, those involved in building it shared a vision and a sense of purpose and timelessness that made their work worthwhile although most of them knew they would not live long enough to see it finished. What counted for them was that they had been part of it, in however small a way.

By afternoon teatime we were in Le Touquet, in the queue for the next twenty-minute air ferry to Lydd, which flew just above the water and took two or three small cars and a handful of passengers at a time. Once we had crossed the Channel we had to drive on the other side of the road, which made roundabouts interesting. Cassie was in charge of the map.

'We want the road to Slug,' she said. 'Not Slug,' I remonstrated. 'It's pronounced "Slough."'

'That's not possible,' she complained. 'You say "enough" so it must be "Sluff," or "Slug" or "Slew" like "through."' She had a logical French mind.

Everything in England seemed cheap to us, coming from Switzerland, but I felt like a foreigner because I no longer understood the jokes people made or their references to English current affairs and politics. People discussed politics a lot more than they did in Switzerland, where everything — a proposed increase in the cost of posting a letter, or a litre of milk was decided by referendum, so everyone felt satisfied they had had their say. Swiss people even had trouble remembering the name of the President of the Swiss Confederation because the incumbent changed every year — each of the seven members of the executive taking turn in order of seniority.

We spent a week with my sister in Denham and a few days in London, sightseeing. As usual we went to Buckingham Palace to stand in front of the guards so that Cassie could try to distract them — in vain. One day I telephoned Mike and Carol who had gone back to live in Beer, East Devon. I hadn't seen them since we parted in the Caribbean and they sailed off in their catamaran, *If Dogs Run Free*, heading for England and home. They had insisted that we go to visit them for a few days so we set off for East Devon.

Mike and Carol gave us a warm, friendly and emotional welcome. It was like coming home. Their house was at the top of a steep cobbled street leading down to a pebbly beach, where their barefoot young son was in charge of a row of fishing boats for hire. They made us feel like celebrities and introduced us to all their friends. Soon people were greeting us wherever we went.

One evening we left Cassie with the neighbours, who had children her age, while we went to the local pub. Portly tweed-clad 'gentlemen-farmers' stood round the bar, talking in loud Devon-accented voices and puffing at their pipes. Carol met some friends and stood outside talking to them while I hovered just inside the door, not sure whether women were allowed inside. Mike pushed his way through to the counter to buy 'scrumpy' which turned out to be quite a different kettle of fish from the apple juice I was used to in Switzerland. Not only was it much stronger tasting and very alcoholic but the glasses were huge. I was not accustomed to such quantities and after a while desperately needed the toilet. That, however, involved pushing my way through the barrier of pipe-smoking men to get to the doorway the other side. I postponed action for as long as I could and then, summoning all my courage and apologising profusely to right and left, I set about forcing my way through the crowd. Once there all I could see was a 'Gents'. No sign of a 'Ladies'. Obviously, I shouldn't have been in the pub at all, it was for men only. Embarrassed, I wondered how I would ever dare go back inside. In the meantime, my immediate problem was to find a 'Ladies' toilet. Everyone I could see had their back to me, so, in desperation, I stealthily tiptoed into the 'Gents'. Along the wall was a row of urinals and, at the far end, a cubicle with a door, into which I darted, hurriedly closing and locking the door. That, however, was not the end of my problem. They had unfortunately only just begun. I could hear men coming in, talking in loud voices and splashing into the urinals. How could I ever be brave enough to come out? Men's toilets are smellier than women's. I hated being there but each time I started to open the door to peep out, I had to shut it again hurriedly because a man's back was just outside, and I could not bring myself to walk confidently past a row of penises on display. Some twenty unpleasant minutes must have passed before there was silence and I could finally escape but just as I reached the outside door a man as large as a wardrobe zoomed in, whistling and unzipping as he went. He looked extremely surprised to come face to face with me in my bright lime-green dress. When I finally re-joined Mike and Carol, they were frantic, wondering where on earth I could possibly have disappeared to.

The following day they took us to Exeter cattle market. I had never seen so many sheep and cows. It was drizzling with rain; huddling together in our raincoats we splashed about in the mud, and horse and cow dung, trying to avoid the pointy bits of one another's umbrellas. Once again, I was wearing the wrong shoes. Auctioneers stood on platforms calling out to the gathered crowds; I stopped on the fringe of one group to watch. The auctioneer called out: 'Lady says thirty,' then 'Seventy to the lady' and Mike explained that I had just bought five sheep. I had touched my hair — a horsefly was buzzing round me. Apparently, that was enough. A nod, a smile or a wave of the hand and you had bought something on four legs. For a few horrible seconds I wondered what I would do with five sheep until everyone burst out laughing and I realised it was a joke traditionally played on unsuspecting visitors.

At home with Mike and Carol we spent the evenings making music, sitting in a circle on the carpeted floor of their lounge-room while Mike sang his songs, accompanying himself on the guitar. There was one in particular entitled *Bequia*, which brought back happy memories. In fact, memories were rather a problem because we couldn't help reminiscing about picnics on uninhabited islands with Peter and thinking about him brought tears to my eyes. I wondered how many letters would be waiting in my green wooden letterbox when I got home.

In fact, among the pile of letters waiting for me was one announcing a heart-stopping piece of news: Peter had to fly to London for work. He would be there for three or four days and if I flew over, we could at least spend the evenings together.

I packed a suitcase with my favourite dresses and smartest high-heeled shoes, then caught a plane to London in a state of great anticipation. My face was flushed, I almost forgot my passport, and the excitement gave me diarrhoea which considerably complicated travel, frequently causing me to forgo my place in queues. Somehow, I nevertheless managed to get to Heathrow.

* * *

When Peter came through the gate at the airport and kissed me, I stupidly started to cry. I couldn't stop myself even though I knew my mascara would run down my face onto my 'Pancake' make-up.

In the evenings we strolled through the London streets, and everything seemed bathed in magic again because we were together. When I said I was tired and my feet hurt — my flimsy, elegant sandals were far from ideal for long-distance walking on unforgiving London pavements — Peter offered to carry me. We struggled there on the pavement while he tried to pick me up and I resisted with all my might, laughing and screaming. In the end he insisted upon taking my shoes off and putting them in the pocket of his mac, making me wear his big black lace-up shoes. I flapped along like Donald Duck while he tiptoed in his socks. Fortunately, night was just beginning to fall.

I had left my contact details with a colleague in Geneva and that evening, lying in bed at the Royal National Hotel, the telephone rang. The call was from New Delhi. Was I free to accept a Non-Aligned Movement conference in Cuba the following week? I had to reply immediately because if I wasn't able to do it, someone else would have to be found and time was short.

I put the phone down on the bedside table. 'Shall I go to Cuba next week?' I asked. Peter's face fell.

'It was meant to be a surprise,' he mumbled 'but I have managed a few extra days and I was hoping we could go to Cowes in the Isle of Wight. That's where my boat, the *Solent Dove*, came from originally.'

'So, what shall I say?' I asked. 'Cuba or Cowes?'

'You'd better accept Cuba,' he said. 'It means a lot of money for you. And it's good for your career.'

I picked up the phone. 'Sorry,' I said. 'I'm not free.' That was that. It would be Cowes.

When we got there, we stayed at the Holmwood Hotel and looked at boats. Then we visited Yarmouth and looked at more boats, then Gosport — Westerly boats — and Chichester for old time's sake and even more boats. We found a restaurant run by an amazingly eloquent 'olde-worlde' Viennese man whose food was excellent. The bread was freshly baked on the premises and hot from the oven. We felt we were in a time warp.

'I wouldn't be surprised if tomorrow we came this way and found this restaurant was no longer here,' Peter said as a small round silver dish of after-dinner mints was placed before us. 'Even these homemade mints are the sort to melt in your mouth and leave no trace. I believe it's all magic.'

Near Ventnor we walked along a footpath into the woods and came across an old house half buried in undergrowth and covered in ivy. It seemed to be abandoned yet in the garage at the end of the garden were two cars, one with the bonnet open and a can of oil left standing on the engine as though the owner had suddenly been called away. Perhaps he had just disappeared in a puff of smoke. Anything was possible in that enchanted atmosphere.

\* \* \*

One day we went shopping in London. I was looking at some frilly lace petticoats and debating in my mind whether to buy one for Cassie. An elegant saleswoman with blonde hair and sparkling eyes said: 'You're a womanly woman. Why don't you buy one for yourself? What's the good of being a woman if you can't dress in feminine frills and lace? I did the washing-up in mine the other evening and you'd be surprised what it did for my marriage!'

So, I bought two: one for Cassie and one for me, though I didn't have time to wear mine before Peter went back, so I never found out what it did for the unmarried. While I was at the cash desk the saleswoman asked Peter if he was my husband. Surprisingly, he said 'yes' and she said something nice about me. Afterwards, sitting on a wooden seat in the park, Peter said very seriously:

'Why aren't you my wife? Can you give me one good reason why you aren't my wife?'

I remained silent. It was rather a big question. Too many people would be upheaved if we got married.

When he saw *Kismet* was on in town, Peter insisted we go to see it; sitting in the back row of the balcony was hot and stuffy but we didn't care. We saw little of the show anyway because we spent most of the time kissing in the dark. We felt about seventeen but in fact Peter was fifty-three then and I was fifty.

After the usual tearful farewell at Heathrow, Peter checking in for a flight to Australia while I was in the queue for Geneva, we suddenly found ourselves back in our other worlds.

I was due at the International Labour Organisation's June conference next morning. I thought of Peter every time the Australian delegates challenged our imagination with their amazing vowels and sometimes baffling Australianisms. I was impressed by Bob Hawke's beautiful head of silvery hair and the fact that, whereas everyone else wore a dark suit and tie to sign the Final Acts of the conference, he came down from his seat to the signing table in white shirtsleeves. He seemed to have a very likeable personality, always smiling, laughing, and making jokes. He impressed the interpreters with his self-confidence and originality. He served on the Governing Body from 1972 until 1980 and was awarded the UN Media Peace Prize in 1980.

After that I had a series of conferences in Rome, Madrid, Bangkok and Yaoundé with only a few days in between, so there was little time to miss Peter.

\* \* \*

I hadn't seen Rocky and Julia since our farewell in Grenada in 1975 when they said they reluctantly planned to head back to New Zealand to resume their everyday lives. I found it difficult to imagine them confined to one place, living everyday lives.

However, Peter mentioned in one of his flimsy aerograms that he had heard over the amateur radio network that they had reached Suva in Fiji and decided to stop there for a while before continuing their trip home. I was overjoyed when I received a telephone offer of an FAO[1] conference in Suva, which meant I would be able to catch up with them

---

1   Food and Agriculture Organisation, headquartered in Rome

again. I knew I would recognise their beautiful, graceful yacht, *Quinquereme*, the moment I caught sight of it.

After a few days I received three large packets of conference documents for each of the committees and working groups, one for each of the three languages. I set about re-familiarising myself with fish habitats among the mangrove roots, wading birds, mosquitoes and wetlands. The conference was to take place at the Tradewinds Hotel where a room had been reserved for me.

The entrance to the hotel was a mass of exotic palms and flowers. I checked in and a bellboy appeared to take charge of my suitcase, placing it on a tall trolley. I followed him through the hotel, out the other side and into the bright sunshine, past the swimming pool and the marina. Then he turned to the left and led me past a row of rooms to the very last one. He unlocked the door and deposited my suitcase on the bed. After he had left, through the open door, about five metres from where I stood, I could see *Quinquereme*, tied to a bollard with invitingly placed heavy ropes, swaying gently from side to side in all its graceful majesty, a plank of wood from its deck to the wharf.

It was a magic moment. I could have wished for nothing more.

Leaving my room door open while I unpacked, I was able to see as soon as there was movement on deck and ran across to say 'hello'. After the cries of surprise and delight and a round of excited hugs, I was invited on board for a welcome drink.

They were still living on board, but Rocky hoped to get a job with a local air-conditioning company in which case they would rent a house in town. He was as tall, long-legged and slim as ever, his head surrounded by the usual golliwog halo of curly, brown hair. He had a long, sensitive nose and a two hundred per cent sparkle in his bright grey eyes. He was never still.

Julia hadn't changed either — she was still the most energetic and independent woman I had ever met, as well as being tall, slim, beautiful, a wonderful cook and photographer.

The following morning when I opened my eyes, blinded by the sun streaming through the chinks between the curtains, I remembered with excitement: the boats! And stepping out on to my balcony, there lay before me a whole array of old friends: *Varua, Cyn-San, Carapace, Quinquereme, Tanoa Suva, Aotahi, Alfreda, Castaway, Sly Grog, Ocean Girl* and *Spellbound* …

A native lady on board *Quinquereme* was hanging washing out to dry. As I approached, she called out: 'Julia will be back at 1 o'clock. She is expecting you.'

On the distant horizon the reef splashed with foam, dazzling white against the turquoise blue of the sea; small islands were dotted here and there, densely packed with dark green trees.

Pausing to look down over the stone wall bordering the hotel grass walkway I could see the most beautiful small dark blue fish darting in and out like brightly coloured birds undulating gracefully through the water, their movements weaving patterns which reminded me of swimming galas in old Esther Williams Hollywood films.

Outside my door, facing the waterfront, was a hibiscus bush with healthy dark green leaves and a profusion of deep-red flowers so red they must be the very essence of redness. As I sat sipping my tea in the doorway something moved in the hibiscus bush: a tiny bird half the size of a small sparrow. It was deep green in colour with a red head and tail …

The conference atmosphere was quite stress-free compared to similar conferences in Europe; the delegates, mostly from the Pacific Islands, wore brightly coloured decorative short-sleeved open-necked shirts and not dark suits, white shirts and ties. They were mostly overweight, relaxed, informal and they smiled a lot of the time. Music seemed to play an important part in their lives — every evening there was island-style dancing and harmony singing in the hotel gardens. The only exception to all this was the Australian delegate who wore at all times a dark suit, plain white shirt and tie. I felt he took 'representing Australia' rather too seriously. He was tall, pale and fair-haired; I noticed that his face got pinker and pinker with each day.

After work I went back to my room and collapsed on the bed. Soon there was a gentle tap on the door: it was Echo, Rocky and Julia's small daughter, sent across to invite me on board *Quinquereme* for supper.

We had wonderful crusty bread with avocado and fish soup so tasty and delicate I felt it was The Perfect Fish Soup. Then we had chocolate ice-cream and baked egg custard, all homemade by Julia on board. Glass in hand we talked long into the night, watching the water ripple alongside and the reflections of all the surrounding boats. We watched the sun set and the moon gradually come up and felt truly at peace with the world.

When I finally went back to my room it seemed impolite to close my door on the smooth sea, shimmering and shining in the moonlight. The masts of the boats could have been in my garden — they were just beyond the narrow strip of lawn: white and blue, all softly asleep, their masts tinkling gently as they swayed in the light breeze.

\* \* \*

I spent as much of my free time as I could with Julia, Rocky and Echo on board *Quinquereme*. Julia produced gastronomic feasts and Rocky was very generous with wine, gin and whisky. We spent many hours, at first, reminiscing about our sailing experiences a few years earlier, and wondering what had happened to all the wonderful people we had met. Most evenings we ended up a little tipsy but very happy — fortunately I didn't have far to go to my room and my bed.

It was the end of the rainy season: an ever-changing mixture of sunshine and rain but always warm and humid. The water rippled and sparkled greenly for we were inside a lagoon and there were islands on all sides at varying distances, all covered with lush green vegetation and mangroves. At night I heard strange bird sounds the like of which I had never heard before: little explosive sounds — I imagined the bird puffing out its chest proudly to make them.

Lilli and Gusti were a couple of Swiss architects from Zurich, living on *Carapace* — a houseboat; they invited Julia, Rocky and me aboard one evening for dinner on deck under the stars. Julia took much of the food, which she had expertly prepared on *Quinquereme*. Gusti was a force of nature, he looked like a Viking and behaved like one. He reminded me of Eric the Red: I could imagine him raising his sword above his head to cut you in two right down the middle, if he took umbrage at something you had said. He was tall and strong and had a regal way of discarding cigarette ends or emptying his glass overboard. His wife, Lilli, on the other hand was tiny, slim, quiet-voiced and delicate. When I mentioned that in Versoix, Switzerland, I had planted a cherry tree to celebrate the birth of each of my three children, Lilli said 'That's a coincidence! Here in Fiji they bury the umbilical cord that drops off the baby after ten days or so; then they plant a tree on top, so each child has its own tree to talk to and each child knows where it truly belongs.'

They told me about a local school where the *sulu* was the compulsory school uniform for boys and, according to Fijian custom, no undergarment was allowed. The shy son of a non-Fijian friend of theirs had been embarrassed because the other boys made fun of him in the playground by lifting up his sulu to make sure he was not wearing underpants; he came home from school in tears day after day until his parents finally had to send him to a different school.

It was hard to believe the gentle people of Fiji had once been cannibals, but Robert Louis Stevenson maintained they still were in the 1890s — not only in Fiji but also in the other islands of the Pacific. Apparently little boys were enticed away by other tribes to be eaten as well as unwanted, lonely fisherwomen, sent off to lonely places far from home where they would be eaten by other passing tribes. Someone said that cannibalism still exists in Papua New Guinea particularly among the Korowai tribe.

*  *  *

The conference lasted only two weeks but at least I had one free weekend in the middle; Rocky and Julia took me to the local market and drove me all over town in their old car introducing me to their many friends. Julia and Rocky loved living in Fiji and seemed to have no plans to leave. The only thing they missed was good coffee — all they could get was the instant variety so I promised to bring them a supply of coffee beans each time I visited Fiji in the future.

The first thing I heard every morning was laughter and joyful squealing as Echo, always up first, dived and splashed in the Tradewinds pool. When I drew open my yellow-orange, sun-dazzled curtains I could see her high up on the flagpole, or climbing across the decorative framework, her slim, lithe brown body shining wet; as soon as she saw me she waved. Then she splashed down into the pool, squealing with joy as she went. She must have been about five, the epitome of health and happiness, the perfect water-baby.

The conference came to an end and we said sad goodbyes. I promised to be back soon: from then on, I would happily accept all offers of work in Fiji and be sure to come well laden with coffee.

Those two balmy weeks at the Tradewinds live in my memory in a radiant glow of happiness.

\* \* \*

The time came at last when Peter had accumulated enough leave for us to take our much-awaited holiday in Greece. I reserved a hotel room in Skiathos with a large balcony overlooking the bay, and we succeeded in booking flights arriving within half an hour of each other in Athens so we would meet in the airport. We counted the days, unable to believe it was really going to happen. Two glorious weeks together on a Greek island!

But two days before departure I had almost finished packing when a telegram arrived:

'Unable to leave for a week or two. Will phone.'

His ex-wife (legally still his wife) had had a car accident

and he had been summoned to the hospital. She was now ready to go home and he had to look after her.

In the end he could manage only the last five days of our planned holiday. By the time we reached our hotel we were both jet-lagged and exhausted from work and travel. I had only just got back from a last-minute conference in Uganda and he had travelled for twenty-seven hours. Our only desire was to sleep. I tried all the tricks I could think of to keep him awake but he nodded off at the most inconvenient times.

We did have the most wonderful, leisurely breakfasts on our balcony though, surrounded by olive trees, looking out over the sparkling turquoise sea. We watched passing ships as we sipped black tea and ate crusty fresh bread still warm from the bakery with rich Greek honey, while bees buzzed all round us in the encroaching branches of a flowering tree. There were beautiful evenings too, in a café drinking ouzo or retsina at square wooden tables while the boats tied up along the wharf tipped lazily this way and that. We climbed to the top of a hill to look at the tiny white monastery and took a boat trip to nearby Lalaria to see a famous rock with a big hole in it and admire the marble-white beach and powder-blue water. We visited unspoilt beaches and swam in the warm aquamarine transparency of the Aegean, walked through leafy forests and little villages inhabited by donkeys, smiling people and huge pots of tumbling geraniums.

By the time Peter had recovered from jet lag his departure was imminent and everything we did and said was drenched in pathos. Whatever beauty we looked at our misery somehow showed through.

'I'll telephone on your birthday,' he promised.

As I settled in my seat on the plane home, I thought that at least I had that to look forward to.

When I got home and walked in the front door, I realised the same flowers were still fresh in their vases as I had left them. It was hard to believe I had been gone at all. At the same time those five days had been so intense they almost felt like a lifetime.

'The desperate quality of middle-aged love,' someone once called it.

* * *

A few months later I received a letter from Peter saying it was about time I went to have a look at Australia. It was true that, like most Europeans, I knew nothing at all about it except that all the Australian delegates I had encountered spoke with a sort of cockney accent, just as I would imagine convicts spoke, and that their vowels had to be heard to be believed. But of the country itself, apart from kangaroos. I knew nothing. Its flora and fauna, or its land and seascapes were unknown.

By a stroke of luck, one of my conferences was cancelled at the last minute which meant that I had a three-week gap, so soon I was once again in a taxi heading for the airport. The flight to Australia seemed interminable — the longest I had ever endured. How could people willingly spend so long in an aeroplane? Surely it was about time someone invented a better and faster system for long-distance travel?

All such thoughts were forgotten when I saw Peter waiting at the airport with a huge bunch of carnations. He had an old white Triumph waiting in the car park — it looked pretty shabby and shaky to me and I wondered whether it could be trusted. In those days I didn't know how much he loved tinkering with old cars, covered in black grease up to the elbows, preferably in the horizontal plane with only his feet sticking out from underneath.

We drove to a serviced apartment he had rented in East Melbourne where there were more flowers, a fridge full of food, a cassette player with a pile of tapes, bars of chocolate, bottles of wine and packets of biscuits. Then he hurried off to work. That evening he called in to let me know he couldn't stay the night because he hadn't told his wife yet that I was there. He said that in future he would do his best to stay. In any case I needed sleep after the long trip.

Our apartment was fully furnished and the cupboards contained plates, cutlery, cups, glasses and a teapot but nowhere could I find a single coffee cup. There were no coffee spoons either and no coffeemaker. Strange. On the other hand, on a row of hooks in the kitchen I noticed a row of attractive, brightly coloured jugs — oddly however with no pouring lip. It was some time before I realised this is what people drank their instant white coffee from: coffee mugs. I had never seen a mug before.

Next day Peter arrived with a suitcase and moved in. After that, when leaving for work in the morning he would tell me where to meet him for lunch in town. In the meantime I explored Melbourne and was greatly impressed by the extensive parks with beautiful trees and flowers unlike any I had ever seen before.

It seemed strange that, in a country so far from England could be so very different.. There were brightly coloured birds, amazing flowers and trees, dazzling sunshine, turquoise sea and white sand, summer heat and water shortages instead of greyness and drizzle. The people sounded and looked just like English people: pale complexions, patches of painful-looking sunburn, white legs and bony knees poking out of their shorts. They drank cups of strong hot tea with milk and sugar as though they needed to keep warm. (In Geneva tea was amber-coloured and came in a tall glass with a slice of lemon.) Oven-baked dinners on Sundays were eaten even on the hottest of days. They spoke like Londoners. The women all seemed to have the same permed hairstyle and similar clothes — mostly tracksuits — with clumsy sensible shoes. They all carried large funereal black handbags. Surely a wallet, a comb, a lipstick and a set of keys would fit into something smaller and more elegant and why not an attractive colour? I often wondered what filled those large, ugly black handbags they carried around with them wherever they went. The atmosphere was Mediterranean but where were the olive groves and the music? Surely people here should be tanned, brown-haired and speak Greek, Italian or Spanish, and sing as they walked along the street.

But for one week I imagined how different Australia would be if the Portuguese or the French had planted their flag first. There would be shaded carparks, no roast turkey and Christmas pudding in the heat of Christmas Day, people would sing as they walked down the street, clean their windows or sweep in front of their houses, and there would be no incomprehensible cricket — something I wouldn't miss at all. I must confess I do not speak 'golf' or 'cricket'. Or 'soccer'. Perhaps there would be *pétanque* (outdoor bowls) under the trees in the cool of the evening ... and no nine-to-five working day. Instead, a delightful, self-indulgent siesta would follow lunch during the hottest time of the day in summer. Later, after work in the cool of the evening, there would be a gentle stroll along the esplanade or in the park, or an ice-cream or coffee in a pavement café with the children who would afterwards play on the park swings, while the eligible maidens and marriageable bachelors looked one another up and down, as they strolled past each other. How could these people eat tasteless square sliced white bread from the supermarket for breakfast when real bread was available from the bakeries and an unappetising something they called 'wheaties' that looked, smelled and tasted like animal feed to me? Then they would work from nine-to-five and go home to eat, then spend the evening watching sport on television in that beautiful sunny Mediterranean climate.

The absence of bidets in bathrooms was another thing that mystified me. How could Australians keep themselves clean without a bidet? They seemed to think an overhead shower was the answer but I did not feel clean unless I could wash myself from underneath as well. In a bidet-deprived country, the only way to wash oneself properly would be to balance on your hands, upside down, under the shower, but that would be rather an unladylike way of solving the problem.

I imagined hand-standing Australians under the shower, early risers at 5 am, lazier ones like me later! Grey long-haired hand-standers, perky young hand-standers, bald obese hand-standers. Over-eighty hand-standers doddering under the warm, comforting spray, wicked old grandmothers chortling as the spray gave them a tingle. The hairy, the skinny, the sporty, the dithery — the new-world no-more-bidet hand-standers of Australia ... a whole new concept.

The only problem with handstands is the rather off-putting thought that, by the time the water reaches your face, you know where it has been before.

If you really don't feel energetic enough to do a handstand under the shower, all you have to do is obtain one of the Swiss-style hand-held variety and your problem is solved. The Swiss have answers to everything, and I am talking from experience.

While on the subject of showers, with or without handstands, there are hundreds of species of skin microbes

(I could even give you their names in Latin[2]) which form a protective shield that we scrub off when we wash our skin. However, this shield protects us, educates the immune system, modulates the immune and inflammatory response, and doesn't allow pathogenic or opportunistic bacteria.

We are thus faced with a dilemma: do we want the best for our microbes while running the risk of social exclusion, or should being pleasant company be our top priority in spite of the wellbeing of our microbes?

For those who are at this moment chortling away as they congratulate themselves on the fact that they take baths instead of showers, may I point out that it would be difficult to imagine a less hygienic method of keeping clean than soaking in one's own dirty water, and among one's discarded skin microbes and dead skin flakes.

Another subject dear to my heart is suppositories. They were used in Ancient Egypt, Greece and Rome as well as by the Hebrews and are mentioned in various ancient texts. They are still used in most European countries, particularly in the case of babies and small children where they are so much easier to administer than swallowed medication. They are immediately absorbed by the rectal mucus into the bloodstream without passing through the

---

2   It is time I apologised for one of my professional defects: I am afraid I have a heap of compost inside my brain, composed of the residue from all the specialised international conferences at which I have interpreted over the years. This useless information rises to the surface from time to time; I regret I am unable to resist the temptation to sprinkle a little of it here and there, now and again.

digestive system and possibly upsetting it. In Europe they are the first medication that comes to mind to treat sore throats and bronchitis. Bringing up my three children in Switzerland, their use seemed perfectly normal, as was taking their temperature the only reliable way: via the anus. (Although Australians delight in insulting one another by referring to them as 'arseholes,' they seem to be in denial, themselves, about possessing an anus at all.) If I raise the subject, they look at me strangely, as if I am suffering from some sort of perversion.

I wonder how mixed marriages cope with this problem. Do they have two thermometers in the house, each with a clear indication of the orifice into which it is to be inserted? I do hope no mistakes are ever made.

I also discovered that in Australia men and women wore uncomfortable and unbecoming elastic-waisted pyjamas. Why don't women wear cool non-restricting nightgowns like European women? How could they bear elastic at their waist in the heat? As for men wearing pyjamas instead of nightshirts — how long will it take them to work out the advantages of the nightshirt?

It was in Australia that I saw my first black swans; I wondered why they were white in one hemisphere and black in the other, and whether along the equator they were half white and half black, perhaps striped? Or simply grey? Similarly with oysters: Why are pearls black in Polynesia and white elsewhere? How does the oyster know which part of the world it is in or is it the piece of grit that knows? I also happen to know (that professional defect again) that lobsters communicate by urinating; is it possible to urinate in different languages? If you put a French lobster among Australian lobsters, would they understand one another?

\* \* \*

While Peter was at work during the day, I would sit on a bench under a spreading tree in the park and muse on all these discrepancies. I missed street fountains. In Italy or France or Switzerland you would buy fruit in the street market and go to the fountain to wash it before eating. Where do you wash your fruit in Australia, or your children's sticky hands and faces when they have eaten ice-cream or a sticky bun? I missed street fountains.

Also lying in bed on a Sunday morning listening to church bells. The thought of all the early risers scurrying off to church somehow enhanced the enjoyment of luxuriating in the welcoming cocoon and indulgent comfort.

Melbourne was crowded because the annual Moomba Festival had just begun and this kept me busy for a few days: there was so much to see. I especially enjoyed the art and sculpture exhibitions and the dancing and singing displays. Sometimes when Peter had finished work, we wandered along the Yarra River to watch the college teams rowing. It was a peaceful atmosphere that reminded me of Cambridge in England. One evening we had dinner on a luxurious boat. We spent our first weekend on the beach

— so much more beautiful, less crowded and polluted than the European ones. The beauty of Australian seascapes took my breath away.

For my last weekend we visited Pambula Beach in New South Wales, ten hours' drive from Melbourne, where Peter's parents lived. Ten hours in a car seemed like a nightmare to me. In Switzerland one hour was a long drive and could take you to another country. You made sure to stop halfway for coffee so you didn't feel sleepy at the wheel. But Peter seemed to think nothing of a ten-hour drive.

'If we do meet any big grey kangaroos on the country roads, we have a kangaroo bar on the front of the car,' he pointed out. This did not reassure me in the least. His first concern seemed to be for the car but I hated the thought of hurting a beautiful kangaroo — I had read somewhere that they have real eyelashes and cry real tears.

Driving all those hours gave me time to reflect on the Australian countryside I was seeing for the first time. The tall, slender gum trees on either side of the road looked as though their trunks were vases; mysterious hands had carefully arranged the branches into them like flowers in a bouquet. The birds were all colours! Apart from the green lorikeets I had seen in India, I had never before seen such beautiful brightly coloured birds: magnificent red, purple, yellow, green, gold and blue and larger ones that were delicate pink and white or white with yellow crests. I would have liked to stop and photograph each and every one. Yet, people took them for granted, and some people we visited inexplicably fed and cared for ugly, raucous beady-eyed magpies instead.

We saw no people or human habitations for miles along the highway and few restaurants. I could say 'none' because the Golden Fleece establishments, often part of the petrol stations we passed, could hardly be called 'restaurants' although that is what the sign outside said. The stomach-churning smell of frying cheap cooking oil assailed one's nostrils from afar, and the food on offer held no attraction whatsoever. I missed the excellent overhead restaurants at regular intervals along the motorways of France, Spain, Italy and Switzerland, accessible from both sides of the road, where a large variety of delicious, healthy food was available.

Fortunately, we had a picnic with us and stopped to eat it in a place called the Cann River which is where I discovered the Australian fly. They descended upon us and our sandwiches in black clouds and no matter how aggressively we chased them away they came back with a determined expression on their nasty little faces. Surely in almost two hundred years it should have been possible to do something about the flies?

The warm, open-armed welcome Peter's mother and father gave me chased away any negative thoughts about flies or anything else; I was amazed at their kindness especially as this was the first time we had met. Their house was homely and welcoming with a breathtaking view of the sea, and a much-loved rather wild garden with huge flowering ginger plants that filled the air with their scent. There were irises, too, drooping white lilies and wattle trees. A large waratah bush stood in one corner, covered with amazing red flowers like small scarlet cabbages that looked as though they came from another planet. Because Peter's parents were both artists the house was full of their paintings: there were no vacant spaces remaining on any wall and in the corners stacks of canvasses awaited frames. Many were of flowers; I found them enchanting.

As I entered the house, the first thing I saw was a blue and white check tablecloth on a round table in the window alcove with a mauve vase of pink and purple asters: a picture waiting to be painted.

The main subject of conversation when we first arrived was how much water remained in their rain tank — a strange and surprising topic to someone coming from Switzerland where water was always plentiful. I had a shock later when I went to the toilet and looking up at me with great curiosity from under the rim of the toilet bowl was the sweet face of a small green tree frog. I decided to postpone. I shall never forget that pretty innocent little frog face blinking its eyes up at me questioningly ...

Peter's father liked to talk about his life as a newspaper editor in Melbourne in his younger days, but now he was slowly dying from emphysema after years of smoking. His mother was amazingly energetic, kind, and the prettiest eighty-year-old I had ever seen. I would never have believed an old lady could look so attractive in her large-brimmed pink straw hat decorated with flowers. She insisted upon driving us round the countryside in the hope of seeing some wild kangaroos — in vain. It was generally assumed that there were over one hundred million kangaroos in Australia yet when I left at the end of my stay, I had still not seen a single one in the wild.

Our bedroom had an open view of the sea and on my dressing table was a vase of welcoming white roses. That night we slept in the same bed Peter had slept in first with his wife and then for two or three years with his new partner. I was number three.

As we sat eating our breakfast on the balcony outside our room the following morning, two butterflies played love-games, fluttering and chasing one another among the flowers. To one side of the steps leading up to the veranda was a small wooden table with a bowl of birdseed and crowds of green, purple and red lorikeets squabbling as they picked at the seeds. Suddenly one would rise in the air, spread its wings and screech because one of them had had more than its fair share. They were a noisy but lively, colourful spectacle. Next to the house was untamed bushland with tall gum trees, flowering wattle and bottlebrush. As we strolled along the overgrown pathway, brightly coloured parakeets suddenly spread their wings and swooped past. It was an exotic scene very different from anything I had ever experienced.

The pristine local beaches were incredibly beautiful, and most amazing of all, never did we come across another human being. No vendors of ice-cream or pralines, no blaring transistor radios. Just the sound of the sea and the screeching of seagulls. There were also strange rock formations to admire and orange montbretia growing everywhere called weeds in Australia. My father used to grow them in a neat row all around the lawn in our garden in England.

I did wonder why they called dinner 'tea' although one drank wine or beer with it. Or why, after a large meal in a good restaurant, people ordered a 'cappuccino'; surely their stomachs were full and a short black would have been more appropriate? To me, cappuccinos were desirable mid-morning when there was more room in my stomach ...

I sampled Australian wines and found them quite drinkable although many reds had too much tannin for my taste — probably due to the sub-tropical climate and the amount of sunshine. Probably due to the summer heat, people drank their white wines much too cold for my liking. So cold in fact, that they had lost their taste altogether.

As an interpreter I have always been fascinated by local sayings in various languages and have made quite a collection over the years. I was delighted to add to it a long list of Australian expressions like 'bathing togs' which made me think of Rudyard Kipling, 'to go crook,' and 'he feels crook,' as well as 'she'll be apples'. I discovered that when people referred to a hotel, they generally meant a pub, and a 'theatre' often meant a cinema, that a chicken was a 'chook' and that I was a 'sheila'. My professional defect reminded me that 'chelas' were 'eunuchs' in India and I wondered if there was any connection.

I learnt, too, that some people were 'whingers' or 'dole bludgers'. That when you offered tea or coffee to someone they generally said, 'yes, thank you' instead of 'yes, please' and that 'it's a steal' meant 'a bargain'. I also heard mysterious expressions like 'fair dinkum,' 'true blue'. Using the word 'paddock' even when there were no horses I found rather picturesque. I heard 'AW-KYE' quite often and while at first I thought it might be Scottish, after a while I decided it must be Japanese since Australia was after all part of Asia. There was also no doubt in my mind that what sounded like 'Siya' was an Anglicisation of some Asian expression, probably Japanese but I must admit that 'to come the raw prawn' remained a mystery.

Soon I was using words like 'stouch,' 'spruiker,' 'skerrig,' 'fair go,' 'dill,' 'piker,' to be a 'galah,' 'arvo,' 'beaut,' 'fair go' and 'dinky di' at first tentatively and then with increasing confidence. I discovered that I was a 'pommie,' that work was 'hard yakka,' and that a telephone conversation could be concluded with 'Gudonya' instead of 'Goodbye'.

I was mystified by the glorification of the battle of Gallipoli: a ninety-one-year-ago horrendous Australian defeat caused by blind obedience to an over-indulged fat cigar-smoking Englishman named Churchill. The whole campaign had been badly conceived and badly executed, some doubts still remaining as to why this particular beach had been chosen in view of its obvious geographical and strategic disadvantages. Countless deaths had been the result so why celebrate it? As the invasion progressed it had become clear that the Allied soldiers could not win, yet the Higher Command the other side of the globe had nevertheless decided that they should dig in and continue to move forward into the gunfire, which seems unforgiveable to me. Surely, after such a disaster it was time to turn the page? What had Turkey done to Australia to justify this fierce invasion of their country from the sea? I felt Australians should be ashamed of their past behaviour in Turkey, apologise and seek forgiveness rather than expect Turkey to provide amenities for commemoration ceremonies each year. Shouldn't Australia concentrate on past victories rather than defeats?

I don't believe any human being has the right to kill any other. However, if I could somehow insinuate myself into a gun manufacturing plant, and I was clever enough, I could fiddle with the gun-making machinery to change the direction of fire so that the shooter was shot instead of the shootee.

*God Save the Queen* played and sung at the end of musical and theatrical performances came as a surprise: Australia didn't have a Queen! I was British and she was my Queen, not theirs! I also heard talk of a man called Ned Kelly who seemed to be a national hero but had in fact been a gun-wielding outlaw, a terrorist wearing a metal niqab. Surely someone also to be ashamed of rather than celebrated.

It was in Pambula that I discovered the amazing beauty of Australian flowers, so different from any I had seen before in any country, although some of them shocked me by their promiscuousness — one might even call it their pornographic appearance: they seemed to flaunt their sexuality. Voluptuous blooms of easy virtue. They were not fussy: Any bird or bee would do, so long as their sexual needs were satisfied.[3] Many had coloured whiskers and seedpods resembling human genitalia, some brown, some hairier than others. After all, what are flowers if not an invitation to sexual intercourse? A means of attracting fertilising insects or birds to carry pollen from one flower to another? The brighter their colours the louder they cry: 'Come and fertilise me!' They wear the most conspicuous colours they can conjure up to make sure they will be noticed. Like teenagers in miniskirts or the shortest of revealing shorts with jewellery attached to various parts of their anatomy. Like the sexual attraction of women's hair, which has to be hidden in a scarf in some cultures, they flaunt their petals as outrageously as they can. Their libido is most blatant in the case of fragrant flowers, unashamedly making themselves as attractive as possible in order to take advantage of their sexual partners by making them light-headed and slightly intoxicated before foreplay. Sex pheromones, an important factor in the choice of a mating partner, have evolved in flowers, which must explain why women spray themselves with their scent.

---

3   Kahlil Gibran writes in *The Prophet*:
    'But it is also the pleasure of the flower to yield its honey to the bee.
    For to the bee a flower is the fountain of life,
    And to the flower, a bee is a messenger of love
    And to both, bee and flower, the giving and the receiving of pleasure is a
        need and an ecstasy.
    People of Orphalese, be in your pleasures like the flowers and the bees.'

It would seem to be an enormous waste of their seductive charms to put flowers in churches! Although it could be said that they provide food for intriguing thought during boring sermons.

I have heard of malevolent blooms, which produce toxin-laden nectar — now there's a devious trap set by the most beautiful, attractive of them all. They produce what has been called 'mad honey' — indeed a far cry from the ancient Greek notion of nectar as the food of the gods!

Some flowers can be quite wicked ...

\* \* \*

We headed back to Melbourne with a picnic hamper thoughtfully prepared by Peter's mother, containing a thermos of strong tea with milk and a box of homemade fairy cakes.

And then it was time for me to leave this bidet-deprived country and we headed back to the airport. After the usual quick airport goodbye: brave face, stiff upper lip, no lingering, we were once again dependent on aerograms. But we were beginning to find they were no longer satisfactory. Being apart was like having a persistent toothache that greeted you when you awoke each morning. The only time it went away was when we were reunited.

\* \* \*

Among the conference offers awaiting me in the green wooden letterbox by the front gate was one from the World Health Organisation. It was for a six-day Expert Committee on cholera taking place three months later in Suva and I hastened to send a telegram of acceptance and stock up on coffee beans.

To my delight, *Quinquereme* was still tied up to the Tradewinds jetty; however there seemed to be no one on board. I learnt from the hotel receptionist that Julia and Rocky now rented a house in town since Rocky had taken an engineering job; Echo was attending a local school nearby and Julia, who had always been a very keen photographer, was now working for the local museum. I put aside the bags of coffee I had brought and waited until someone appeared on *Quinquereme*.

This eventually happened and after welcoming squeals of surprise and joy, we caught up on our news and relaxed over a few glasses of wine on deck. It was good to be part of their relaxed *yachtie* group once again.

Sun-tanned Julia took me to the market early before work one morning and introduced me to Fijian vegetables and fruit, later showing me how to cook palm hearts ('chonta,' 'palm cabbage,' 'swamp cabbage' or, my favourite, 'burglar's thigh'), which is a vegetable harvested from the inner core and growing bud of certain palm trees.

Every conference I have ever attended in Fiji began with some sort of kava or Yaqona-drinking ceremony. Actually, it tastes rather unpleasantly like Milk of Magnesia; one has to drink it out of the same coconut shell as everyone else present, which does go against the Anglo-Saxon grain. However, one feels obliged to respect the tradition for fear of being impolite or disrespectful. I must confess that so far and to the best of my knowledge I have never had any ill effects, even when, instead of the *yaqona* sold in general stores in little brown paper bags, the authentic version was served, the roots having first been chewed by certain rather overweight local gentlemen. Originally, I was told, virgins did the chewing but these days chewing virgins are few and far between. The resulting mess was then spat out into a large wooden bowl and offered to us, the honoured guests.

It is, in fact, neither alcoholic nor narcotic but soporific with a calming effect, causing numbing of the lips and tongue; it is also used in medicine to treat urinary tract infections, back pains and insomnia. Where men drink it there are fewer fights, everything slows down and there are quite a few silly smiles.

Most conferences I have attended in Fiji have also had a fire-walking show. To be able to walk on fire it is best, apparently, if you are a member of the Sawau tribe, who inherited this ability because one of their ancestors once saved an eel, which turned out to be a spirit god. It only works, also, if the Sawau are feeling happy and have refrained from eating coconut (which is usually their staple diet) and having anything at all to do with women for two weeks beforehand. They must not paint their faces with charcoal, or they will be burnt. Preparations begin two or three days ahead of time when the chosen firewalkers prepare the wood, logs and stones.

They must show the fire they are not afraid of it; they therefore walk calmly and unhurriedly across the pit covered with red hot stones. The secret is self-confidence; they must smile and look self-assured, keeping close to one another and holding their hands up in triumph as they reach the other side of the pit.

On one occasion I stepped forward to be the first to touch the soles of their feet and to my utter amazement they felt cold — colder than my own.

This particular conference was pleasant and easy-going: I knew most of the delegates from past meetings so there was a deal of catching up to do and we spent much time reminiscing over coffee. My interpreter-colleague, Jean-Daniel, was also an old friend — a kind, generous man. He began by giving me a copy of the glossary he had prepared which was unusually thoughtful and generous. Most interpreters keep their precious glossaries to themselves, the fruit of many hours of painstaking homework.

We spent pleasant hours each day after work relaxing on board *Quinquereme* and chatting with Rocky and Julia over a glass of wine.

Among the conference delegates was a very self-assured middle-aged Frenchman I had never met before. His aftershave was particularly potent; he made a beeline for me at every opportunity. As I came out of the booth for the coffee break, there he was — waiting. He mentioned later that he knew I was 'available' because of the silver chain I was wearing round my ankle — a present from Cassie for my birthday. Unfortunately, when putting it on I had no idea which ankle meant you were 'taken' and which meant you were 'free'.

A note from Rocky awaited me at the hotel reception desk saying he would pick me up that evening at seven to take me to dinner in their new home.

A group of delegates and staff were also going into town to dine at a special restaurant that evening and a minibus had been hired to take them there. At five minutes to seven everyone gathered in the hotel foyer to await transport. I was sitting on a bench in the lobby, waiting for Rocky and surrounded by cholera experts, when the French doctor espied me. He was a tall, rather hefty man; he pushed his way across and squeezed in beside me, assuming I was going with the group. We made polite, trivial conversation — he obviously thought he had his evening made. If he stuck to me like glue and paid for my dinner everything would go the way he wanted — he didn't even need to ask.

Suddenly a car drew up outside with a screech of tyres and out stepped Rocky. Tall and slimmer than ever in a skinny white tee-shirt, his long legs encased in skin-tight jeans, he was a striking figure as he came through the glass door, his hair the usual ball of frizz. As usual, he was never still for a moment. There was a sparkle in his bright grey eyes and somehow, he looked the very antithesis of a conference delegate accustomed to sitting for long boring hours, wearing a dark suit and uncomfortable tie. Rocky looked the sort of person who chose to do only the things he liked. The moment he saw me he stopped and, with an enormous smile on his bright face, there in the middle of the hotel lobby he performed a scarecrow dance, hopping from one foot to the other, knees up, then long legs out sideways, feet pointing outwards; a Rocky-style two-knee hop.

The conference delegates looked on in amazement. Here was a spontaneously happy man who didn't care what people thought. Obviously not a man who spent eight or more hours a day sitting in electric light listening to people droning on about cholera research. I jumped up from my bench and ran towards him; we put our arms round one another in a gigantic hug and he danced me round and round in a circle and then out of the door, into his car, laughing. Behind us I could hear the gasp of the French doctor whose evening had just collapsed ...

✩ ✩ ✩

When Peter and I discovered we were both going to the same radiocommunications conference in Kyoto, Japan, our joy knew no bounds, though we did our best to hide our excitement from our colleagues; I made a great effort to keep a happy expression off my face for fear people might ask questions.

The conference building in Kyoto was magnificent and looked out onto a boating lake with shiny gold and red fish darting about in the water. It was surrounded by weeping willows and a park where Japanese couples met to walk decorously in the shade of the trees. Sometimes they actually dared to hold hands but not often — the girls appeared to be very shy. They were pale-skinned and wore or carried large-brimmed hats and parasols; they were dressed in full skirts and lacy tops like delicate dolls and gave the impression of being coquette but on their best behaviour.

The inaugural ceremony of the conference took place in the late afternoon and was followed by a magnificent reception. I wore a long empire-line honey-brown georgette dress and Erika, my interpreter-colleague and booth-mate, said I looked like Marie-Antoinette. All round the hall were decorated stands with chefs in tall white hats and striped aprons offering different types of food, including my favourite *tempura*. On the stage, musicians played and dancers performed amazing acrobatic feats with sticks and yoyos, bells and drums. Every type of drink you could think of was available. The perfumed women guests wore silks, furs and amazing displays of jewellery and the men smelt of expensive aftershave. Walking round the room greeting the people I knew, so many different French perfumes wafted my way that I felt quite intoxicated. Peter and I tried to avoid one another in public but across the room our eyes kept meeting. Later the most spectacular firework display I had ever seen took place outside over the lake; we felt invisible in the dark so we dared to sit close together on the steps of the building, our knees touching, his arm round my shoulders. We ooh-d and aah-d with everyone else at each new dazzling, colourful explosion in the sky. The finale was the title of the conference, lit up in fireworks, sparkling and exploding in all directions.

The following day the conference began and proceeded as usual: plenary assemblies, committee meetings and working groups. Whenever we could meet without being seen we discussed how we would spend our first weekend, finally deciding we would go off somewhere on an adventure. I wanted to stay in a *ryokan*, a Japanese-style hotel, as I had on previous trips to Japan — living the Japanese way was like being on a different planet. We decided to take the Shinkansen — the new bullet-train — to a little country village for the weekend. We wouldn't plan it too much beforehand or make any bookings, just jump off the train when we found a place that appealed to us.

The weather was very hot and in preparation for our trip I bought myself an elegant white *broderie anglaise* parasol with a frill round the edge. (Sunhats always seem to make my head even hotter.) I loved my new elegant parasol and it matched the white cotton dress I planned to wear.

On Saturday morning we were up before anyone else and off to the train station. We queued at the ticket counter, but when our turn came, no one spoke English. We didn't know the names of the train stations or where we wanted to disembark, but in the end we somehow managed to get tickets to somewhere.

The beautiful, modern, streamlined bullet-train was absolutely silent and ran so smoothly not a drop spilt from our brimful coffee cups even though the speedometer on the buffet car wall read 200 km/h. Through the windows we glimpsed a series of traditional scenes: rice farmers in broad-brimmed straw hats, ancient-looking villages and tall birds on stilt-like legs wading in ponds.

When the train stopped at Kurashiki with its canal bordered by weeping willows like a Renoir painting, we instantly agreed this was the place we were looking for and jumped off the train with our shoulder bags. Walking hand in hand down the main street of the little town we found a coffee shop with windows full of brightly coloured plastic replicas of the food and drinks available. No one spoke any English anywhere — all the signs were in Japanese only — but we pointed to what we wanted and sat down to a pleasant coffee with a strange fish-tasting salty pastry. Later, a little further down the street, we came upon the iron gates of an art gallery with placards advertising an Impressionist art exhibition — a wonderful surprise. Here we spent a happy hour or two, smiling at people we met who bowed and smiled back. Wherever we went we were the only non-Japanese faces.

Passers-by constantly stopped to ask if they could take our photograph. Some wanted to practise their English and we were frequently asked, especially by groups of schoolchildren, 'What is your name?' When we answered they giggled and that was the end of the conversation — those four words seemed to be the sum total of their English.

Eventually we came across a *ryokan* and checked in. Our beds were tatamis — rice-straw mats about two centimetres thick — on the wooden floor. My dressing table was at floor level — I could only see in the mirror if I sat on the ground. The half-sized tissue box produced half-sized tissues. We decided to try the very hot Japanese bath and waited timidly until everyone else had left. Then we bravely went through the doorway and the attendant gave us each a towel the size of a small teacloth. The water was very hot indeed and there was a lot of steam which was reassuring because we had never bathed together naked before. Afterwards, dressed in the kimonos provided, we had dinner at a low table in our room. I slept surprisingly comfortably on the tatami with a wooden neck rest: a block of wood as thick as a brick with a neck-sized semicircle removed in the centre at the top, where you rested your head. If you slept on your back, your hairstyle was perfectly intact the next morning. In fact, if you happened to have a complicated interwoven Japanese *chignon*, you would probably only need to brush it once a week, if that ...

Breakfast in the restaurant the following morning was rather embarrassing because we were not prepared for such hospitality. A hostess was allocated to each table and the moment we had finished our fish, rice and vegetables she smilingly refilled our bowls. We were a little overwhelmed until we realised, we had to stop eating at some point and needed to be assertive. Assertive in a very polite way, of course, with a lot of bowing.

Accustomed as I was to wearing unforgiving, leather high-heeled shoes, I loved the Japanese way of leaving your street shoes outside and relaxing in comfortable house-slippers the moment you entered the ryokan. Also, you didn't have to approach the toilet door at the end of the corridor with stealth, trying the handle as quietly as possible to see if someone was inside, because from afar you could see the pair of slippers outside, their owner having hygienically changed into the toilet slippers inside. I was particularly fascinated by the little jump combined with a twisting hip movement required to get your feet out of the corridor slippers, leaving them facing in the opposite direction, ready for when you came out of the toilet. It seemed everyone was an expert at it except me. Unfortunately, try as I might, I was never lucky enough to actually witness anyone performing this acrobatic twisting and jumping.

We were sorry to leave romantic Kurashiki and the ryokan. We had supper on the train and were back in Kyoto far too soon.

My Japanese colleagues at the conference told me about the new water-saving device in ladies' public toilets that had recently been installed everywhere in Tokyo. Japanese ladies were embarrassed to use the toilets if anyone else was in a nearby cubicle because of the possibility of unladylike noises. The Japanese Water Board discovered during a water saving campaign that twice as much water was used in the ladies' as in the men's toilets because the ladies turned the taps on full blast so that the sound of rushing water would create a sound barrier. This led them to a brilliant solution: a sound recording of rushing water which started to play the moment you closed the cubicle door — it was rather like standing next to a giant waterfall. An enormous saving in water consumption was achieved, and the ladies felt perfectly comfortable and uninhibited.

That was the beginning: nowadays beside the toilets in most hotels is a whole dashboard of switches and buttons to enable the user to obtain a dozen different effects — unfortunately this is all explained in Japanese only. There are also two lavatory seats, one on top of the other, separated by springs. The moment you sit on the top seat, you are deafened by the sound barrier. Then, the various possible effects that you can choose from include a bidet-type water spray, water pressure control and even revolving the toilet seat so that it can be disinfected automatically. I have never been brave enough to try revolving it while seated but I am keeping that up my sleeve for a rainy day. It must, no doubt, be an unforgettable experience.

The bath had a moat round it like a medieval European castle, leading to a drain, in case of overflow. They have thought of everything.

In the toilets in Narita airport the lid rises automatically as you enter the cubicle, but if you don't sit down very quickly it takes you by surprise and could be quite dangerous. It closes a few seconds later, amid flashing lights and many rather confusing electronic beeps.

My colleague also explained that traditional Japanese houses, made of timber and paper, were much healthier to live in than western houses because they used no paint which, she said, 'everyone knows is bad for rheumatism and causes damp.'

Kyoto had more than two thousand temples and shrines to visit at weekends — fortunately this was a six-week conference — its grand, historic architecture was undamaged by World War II.

A conference cocktail party hosted by one or other delegation took place most evenings; sometimes a group of us went out on the town after work to the 'MayBe Pub' or to a nightclub. The cabaret shows were very pure, very innocent: girls traditionally dressed in white kimonos with very little skin showing danced and sang, accompanying themselves on a Japanese guitar. They also, apparently, told jokes. Doubtless very proper jokes. But we weren't paying attention — Peter and I were in a world of our own. Often, when we got back to the hotel, we were so happy we did high-kicks all the way along the long corridor between our rooms, giggling and trusting that none of the conference delegates in the rooms we passed would hear us and recognise our voices or open their door.

The conference excursion to Nara was romantic in spite of the 34-degree heat — I was glad I had my beautiful white parasol with me. We visited many temples and wandered through the Zen garden, hand in hand, hoping no one would notice. That evening, back in Kyoto, we joined a group of delegates and interpreters dining in a smart waterside Japanese restaurant sitting on two-inch thick cushions on the floor, not far from 'Rubbers Rane'[4], as Erika called it — a quiet shady street which was the haunt of local couples. The reflections of dozens of decorated paper lanterns all round us shimmered in the water as we sat uncomfortably on the floor and struggled with our chopsticks. A Japanese hostess in a beautifully embroidered kimono knelt on the floor between us at our table cooking the *sukiyaki* and refilling our sake glasses until, having had too much and overcome by the romance of the occasion, Peter bent and kissed my toes that were sticking out underneath the table just next to him. This rather shocked the Japanese diners around us and we felt it was time to leave.

One evening the Australian delegation was invited by the President of a Japanese company to a cocktail party in their high-rise offices. I too was invited — I seemed to have become an honorary member of the Australian delegation. All the men were sampling Japanese beer. Now I am afraid I have never been able to drink beer since I gave birth to my three babies in Switzerland; the sergeant-major

---

4   The difficulty Japanese speakers have in distinguishing between 'l' and 'r' led to another problem. Among the US delegates was a Mr Nicholson and one of the Australians was a Mr Nichols. It was hard for us to keep a straight face each time the Japanese Chairman gave the floor to 'Mr Knickerson' or 'Mr Knickers.' Fortunately, no elections were held.

Swiss-German nurses insisted I drink two litres of beer every day to ensure my milk supply. A two-litre jug of beer was placed on my bedside table every morning with the instructions that I had to have drunk every drop of it by lunchtime.

So, when the President honoured me, the only non-Japanese lady present, by asking me first what I would like to drink, I asked for a gin and tonic. The eyes of the inexperienced young waiter taking the order seemed to fill with panic. At length he reappeared with a tray bearing a large glass, which he then proceeded to fill almost to the brim with gin, topping it off with a splash of tonic water.

Aghast, I stared at the glass and then desperately looked around the room for Peter to come to my rescue. I spotted him laughing and chatting with a group of Australians over a glass of beer on the far side of the room — completely oblivious to my plight. Surely, I thought, after we had been so close, he must be receptive to my ESP panic messages. Apparently not. Everyone was being so polite and there was so much bowing I despaired of ever attracting his attention. I knew where my duty lay: I had to drink what was in my glass for the honour of Australia and to ensure the President of the company did not lose face.

I took a tiny sip, then another.

As I continued distractedly chatting to the President and taking sips of almost neat gin, someone took our photograph. Happily, I have never seen that picture but the flash of the camera drew Peter's attention at last. I was beginning to perspire and the room was spinning round me. Daintily I continued sipping until I started swaying on my feet. Mercifully Peter hurried over and took my arm.

'I'm not feeling well, please take me back to the hotel,' I whispered. Peter grabbed my elbow firmly and after a few polite words to the President we headed for the revolving glass doors that led out of the reception area and Peter pushed me forward into one of the glass compartments.

Once I was safely in, the problem was how to get out. I tried to lurch in the right direction each time we came to the opening and I could see the escalator outside but by the time I had organised myself to take action, the moment had passed and we were revolving again. This went on for a while until Peter, now outside, managed to pounce in time, grab me and drag me out. After that there were the escalator and the lift to negotiate, the taxi, the hotel lift and finally the long corridor, lined with the rooms of conference staff and delegates, along which Peter had to drag me, doing his best to muffle my giggles. When I finally collapsed on my bed, he desperately mopped my forehead with a wet towel, doing everything within his power to stop me singing (which apparently, I was very keen to do), because he knew that if anyone recognised my voice, my reputation and future interpreting career were at stake. To his great relief I suddenly fell asleep and he was able to creep out and tiptoe back to his own room.

My most cherished memory of the Kyoto conference is of our lunchtimes. On the top floor of the conference building was a staff cafeteria where everyone went for lunch — everyone, that is, except for Peter and me. We had a much better plan and every detail of those lunchtimes is etched in my mind like a living, breathing photograph.

Towards the end of the morning, during my free half-hour I would slip out of the booth and take the lift up to the cafeteria to buy food for our picnic. The Japanese food was mysterious but the uncertainty added an element of adventure. I once chose a selection of pretty little parcels wrapped up in brightly coloured paper, twisted at each end like chocolates or toffees. I thought we would enjoy them for dessert but they turned out to be Bombay Duck — sour salt cod strips.

With my dainty Japanese carrier-bag of food and drink at my feet, the moment the chairman announced, 'The meeting will now adjourn until 2 o'clock.' I hurried out of the booth and down the stairs to where Peter was waiting by the boatshed outside the building. We'd jump into a hired rowing boat and he'd row us off. The man in the boatshed began to recognise us after the first few days and gave us a knowing smile as he prepared our boat and passed me my parasol once I was installed on the seat.

The lake was still and green with the reflections of the trees. Occasionally there would be a ripple as a fish came to the surface, snatched a passing insect and disappeared again in the depths. We tried different weeping willows until we found the one, we liked best and after that we made a beeline for it every lunchtime. There, in our own private green world in the seclusion of the willow branches, we unpacked our picnic. Very little was said — there was no need for words. The gently rippling water and the silence, with only the occasional passing family of ducks to disturb us, created a serene problem-free world; once again we felt we were in a time warp. After lunch it was siesta time in the bottom of the boat, but it had to be a 'one-eye-on-the-clock siesta' for I had to be back in the booth without fail by five minutes to two.

At the end of the six weeks, it was even harder than usual to say goodbye. I was never quite prepared for the sudden transition to my other world, or for its finality. My friend and colleague, Erika was heading back to America and discovered she was on the same flight as Peter; she made bright well-meaning conversation as we dragged ourselves around Kyoto airport with long faces.

'Don't you worry, I'll look after him,' she comforted me. 'I'll get a seat next to him on the plane. Is there anything you want me to say on your behalf?' She was a good friend indeed.

I managed to stammer 'No thank you' through the tears and we parted in opposite directions. Geneva and Australia had never felt so far away from each other.

\* \* \*

My next meeting was for the World Food Council in New Delhi and then I was off to Madrid for a meeting on hydrology.

Sitting by the window in so many aeroplanes, gazing out endlessly at the clouds beneath, I daydreamed about bionic aircraft: more supple, more sinuous, more aerodynamic like birds' supple bodies adapting to air currents and taking advantage of thermals. Surely, they would travel faster, with less friction and consume less fuel if their outer surface were less rigid and implacable and more sinuous and adaptable? And wouldn't the transit of ships, too, through water be smoother and require less power if their outer surface were more sinuous and adaptable like that of the body of a fish? The passenger compartment would have to be a separate, habitable area inside, like the womb inside a woman's body.

\* \* \*

After that, I had a string of radio communications conferences in Geneva. I often shared the English booth with Arian, who worked from Russian. A gentle, quiet, polite, kind man with bright blue-grey eyes and pale hair, he was erudite and pleasant to work with. He had diabetes unfortunately and found it difficult to read the conference documents without his glasses plus a large magnifying glass. He also walked with a stick and had trouble negotiating the narrow staircase which led up to our booths in the central meeting room. He never complained however, and somehow managed to cope provided the wastepaper basket under the bench was empty so that it could be turned upside down and he could rest his aching feet on it. At coffee breaks I took his coffee up to the booth to save him having to tackle the stairs.

Arian and his girlfriend, Astrid, shared a cottage in Wales when he wasn't travelling somewhere interpreting at a conference.

We found ourselves working together again in Nigeria soon after, but Lagos was not a pleasant place to be in. There were tales of corruption and taxi drivers were afraid to talk to us as we drove along for fear their taxis had been bugged.

When I first arrived, my taxi from the airport sped through many small villages. Crossing a crowded square in one of them I shall never know whether I really saw — or imagined — a row of men standing with tyres round their necks on chains from an overhead timber frame. Their heads came through the tyres and their hands and feet were roped together.

My five-star hotel was similar to all the other five-star hotels I have stayed in all over the world, two or three dining rooms serving international food, a luxurious swimming pool, an African dance show after dinner in the evenings and a beautiful unspoilt beach which we had little opportunity to enjoy.

We were warned to keep our handbags under our arms at all times and never put them down or leave them out of sight. Street muggings were common so we were advised to stay mostly inside the hotel.

When I think of Lagos now, I remember the first Arian's mugging but then my mind jumps to the Pineapple Ladies.

Throughout the conference, as soon as the Chairman banged his gavel and announced that we would break for lunch everyone rushed to the cafeteria to join the queue. However, the sandwiches and cakes that accompanied our morning coffee and afternoon tea were so lavish that I felt no need for lunch. Instead, I headed down to the deserted beach and installed myself comfortably in a deck chair with a book. No sooner was I seated than three Pineapple Ladies would appear on the horizon and undulate towards me. Tall, slim and indescribably elegant, they had glossy black skin and perfect bodies draped in brightly coloured fabric, which enhanced their silhouette without drawing attention away from it. Their hair was dressed with multiple partings in a pattern which must have taken a while to achieve and plaited with great artistry. On top of it all they bore a round tray piled high with ripe pineapples. The first time I watched them approach with admiration — I believe I had never until that moment appreciated the graceful way African men and women move. One of them knelt at my feet and asked me in an unknown tongue, with a beautiful smile, if I would like some pineapple.

When I nodded 'yes,' I was privileged to witness the deft peeling, slicing and dicing of a pineapple I had ever seen and all so fast I was dumb with admiration. For a few humble coins I had the most delicious lunch imaginable.

As the days went by, we became good friends; the three ladies took it in turns to serve me amid many shy smiles and I looked forward to seeing them each lunchtime.

As I watched them leave and walk down the beach in hopeful search of another pineapple eater, I marvelled once again at the elegance of their gait and noticed how different their bottoms were from the European variety. Theirs were more highly placed, rounder and tighter. As they walked you could see the muscles working; their skirts hung differently from ours as they gracefully undulated along the sand.

I have since given some thought as to why their anatomy is so different from ours and have come to the conclusion that our bottoms are bigger and flabbier because we spend so much time sitting, squashing them out of their natural shape. I believe African women sit rarely on a chair or similar hard surface — on the rare occasions I have seen them in anything resembling a sitting position they were in fact squatting on their haunches, which is quite a different position, developing different muscles. What we European-bottomed women — and men too perhaps — need is a sort of bottom bra. Why do we only scaffold our breasts? Surely bottoms count too! Perhaps one day in the future ladies will wear bottom bras.

In those days, muggings were common in Nigeria so we ate most of our meals in the hotel. However, on our last night we decided to respect the interpreters' tradition: we booked a table at what we were told was the best restaurant in town. If we stayed in groups, sharing taxis from door-to-door, surely no harm could come to us. We had a fine dinner, laughed a lot and dispelled any remaining conference tensions, but Arian was tired and wanted to leave early. It was only later when we left the restaurant that we discovered what had happened to him. A short distance down the road were the flashing lights of a police car and an ambulance. As Arian had crossed the road outside the restaurant to the taxi rank, he had encountered three young Nigerian men walking towards him, arms linked. Apparently, a well-dressed European man walking slowly with a stick was an obvious prey. He had been mugged, his pockets had been emptied and he had been punched in the face and left lying face down on the road. But that was not all. Both of his vulnerable feet had hit the kerb and been injured.

Fortunately, he had medical insurance; he was put on a plane as soon as possible and sent to a hospital in Germany specialising in diabetic problems.

I learnt later that both feet had had to be amputated.

When I got home at the end of the conference, the newspaper headlines told horrific stories of events that had taken place while I was in Lagos but about which I knew nothing. Nuns had been forced to parade in the streets with their breasts cut off, white men had been forced to walk through the streets with their excised genitals in their mouths, escorted by machine-gun carrying Nigerian soldiers ... Switzerland had never felt so safe and welcoming.

I had a string of conferences in Geneva including that of the

International Labour Organisation which took place every year in June, and for which I was regularly booked a year ahead. The delegations came from 151 Member countries and we were 250 simultaneous interpreters working into and out of Arabic, Chinese, English, French, German, Japanese, Russian and Spanish. Our working days were composed of tripartite matters, collective bargaining, guaranteed annual wage, grievance procedures, free riders, fringe benefits, escalator and escape clauses, employers' liabilities, dismissal compensation, disputes, dead time, bumping, stool pigeons, yellow dog contracts, wild-cat strikes, fellow-travellers, lock-outs and lay-offs, unified penal and common codes, indictment, subrogation, voluntary assignments, arbitration agreements, intellectual property laws, and mandatory provisions — in all of those languages.

Before each plenary meeting, 'non-meetings' were held in small rooms all over the building, at which interpretation was required. It was at these non-meetings that strategies were discussed by the various parties concerned: 'If country X does this, we will do that.' 'If delegation Y says that, we will all oppose the original proposal.' 'If delegate Z says so-and-so, we will get up and walk out of the meeting.' It was almost like a game for us, from our interpretation booths, knowing what was likely to happen in each set of possible circumstances but, of course, we had to be careful not to betray what we knew by our tone of voice.

Thus, from one pre-plenary non-meeting I knew that if the UK said something or other, the Australian delegation would walk out of the meeting. And this is exactly what happened.

The Australian delegation, consisting of six or seven men, rose to its feet as one man and filed out of the room, heads held high, behind Mr Hawke.

They gathered at the coffee bar and were soon laughing and joking over their *café croissant*.

Wisely, of course, they had left behind a spy, a friend from another delegation, who popped out from time to time to keep them informed about what was happening in the meeting. So, when discussion began on an agenda item in which the Australian delegation wished to participate, some fifteen minutes later, they abandoned their coffee cups and hastened back into the plenary, in single file behind Mr Hawke as before, and resumed their seats.

The UK and Australia enjoyed exchanging banter whenever they could, and the Chairman was no exception.

'I thought the Australian delegation had left the room in a huff,' he commented.

Mr Hawke rose to his feet.

'Not at all, Mr Chairman,' he said. 'Everyone needs to go sometimes.'

And the meeting continued.

I loved working in the old ILO building because the meeting rooms had real windows and from my booth I could see outside: blue sky, an old oak tree and often a beautiful brown horse standing in its shade. I am sure the quality of my performance was greatly enhanced by this view. Most modern conference venues had no windows. It seems architects think that windows detract from one's concentration, and that seeing the sky or a tree would be a distraction. They should try boring simultaneous interpretation. Quite the opposite is true.

The closing session took place in a circular auditorium; the delegations were seated on rising slopes all round a central area where the signing table was situated, presided over by the Chairman of the conference who signed the Final Acts, followed by each country's representative in alphabetical order, who came down the steps to add his signature. It was always a formal occasion; all the delegates wore a dark suit, white shirt and tie on this day — with the exception, of course, of the leader of the Australian delegation: Bob Hawke, in shirtsleeves. The interpreters found this endearing. He wasn't just a delegate — he was also a man and it was, after all, the end of June and summer had arrived.

It was a few months before Peter came to Geneva again. This time he no longer stayed at the delegation hotel but came to stay with me in Versoix. I took him cross-country skiing in the nearby mountains; once we skied on a frozen lake that we had admired the previous summer surrounded by wildflowers. He was amazed at the thickness of the snow on the chalet rooftops and the size of the stalactites hanging from them.

In the spring we drove to the other end of the Lake to explore the Château de Chillon, the subject of Byron's poem about the prisoner incarcerated in the dungeon. We bent to touch the marks his chains had made on the stone pillars there. In another part of the Chateau I showed him the display of chastity belts — large, heavy and clumsy. How eager the ladies concerned must have been to see from afar their crusader-lovers returning, their horses kicking up the dust as they approached, brandishing a rusty key ...

Peter wanted us to go camping for the weekend. Apparently, it was very Australian to go camping. I couldn't see the point of sleeping uncomfortably on the hard ground in a tent when there were plenty of hotels around with soft beds and real bathrooms with hot showers. However, it seemed important to him, so I finally agreed to try.

Fortunately for me the whole thing was a fiasco, so I never had to go camping again. We loaded our tent, cooking utensils, blankets and pillows and some food into the boot of my little turquoise Fiat 600 and departed in adventurous mood. We hadn't gone very far, however, when it started to rain — at first gently, then more and more heavily. In fact, it didn't stop raining for the whole of the two days. Bravely we tried to fry sausages over a campfire in the rain under a tree, but it was difficult while holding an umbrella. Night fell very quickly — sooner than we expected — and we had to erect our tent by torchlight. My British stiff upper lip, shoulder to the wheel, came in handy throughout.

Our sleeping bags were damp to start with but we slept

in them anyway — we had no choice. During the night, I realised that mine was sopping wet and so was I. Peter had gone outside for a few moments but had not zipped up the flap properly when he came back because it was dark, he couldn't see, and he was half asleep.

All in all, as disasters go, it was pretty successful. I couldn't have wished for better.

* * *

One evening in Geneva we decided to have dinner in a typically Swiss restaurant — the Carnotzet on the Place de la Navigation. This is the sort of place you go to on a cold winter evening — inside a log fire was burning and the air smelt invitingly of melting cheese and white wine. The walls and ceiling were honey-coloured pine, as were the tables and seats, and the tablecloths, napkins and curtains were all red and white check. Swiss mountain music was playing in the background — the sort of clompy Swiss waltzes on the accordion that skiers dance to in the evening after dinner, thumping their heavy boots as they swing their partners round, their faces glowing with warmth, the exercise and the wine after a day in the cold, crisp mountain air.

Fondue is a delicious steaming Swiss speciality made with a mixture of cheeses (which have to be in the right proportions), melted in white wine with plenty of garlic. It is guaranteed to warm the very cockles of your heart. The *caquelon* is placed in the centre of the table on a small spirit heater and you spike a piece of bread on your long fondue fork, dip it in the melted cheese mixture and stir a few times before eating so that the cheese does not catch on the bottom of the pan and burn. Everyone must stir clockwise; tradition has it that otherwise the fondue will not "take" and a failed fondue is a sorry sight for the cheese turns to rubber. If you have not secured the bread firmly on your fork and it falls off into the caquelon, you are the one who buys the next bottle of white wine. Half way through the fondue, *'le trou normand'* (the Norman hole) means that everyone downs a glass of kirsch to provide the stomach with the strength to digest the second half of the fondue. All this is absolutely delectable provided it is accompanied by plenty of Vaudois white wine and not followed by ice-cream or anything cold for dessert, which would turn the cheese into solid concrete inside you.

The other speciality served in a *carnotzet* is *raclette* where the big round cheese is cut in half with a wire and placed close to the heat until the surface melts. Then the soft layer is scraped off and placed in a curl on your plate, together with a gherkin, a small white onion and a potato cooked in its skin (or *robe de chambre* (dressing gown) as some say instead of *robe des champs*). Each plate has a number painted on it; when you have finished you hand back your plate for another helping. A large number of helpings is considered normal for a man — less than that and you are a wimp, more and you are a glutton. I'm not sure whether the required number of helpings is seventeen or whether that is the number of glasses of vodka a true man has to down and still remain standing in Russia. Fortunately, ladies are exempt from these quotas.

We noticed a table of five dark-suited men near us, all looking weary and bored. One of them we recognised as Bob Hawke, who was again in Geneva for a Labour conference — he wouldn't have known, but he had been listening to my voice in his earphones all day. His companions looked like elderly diplomats from India, Africa, and Japan. It was obviously one of those formal diplomatic dinners to which conference delegates are prone. As the evening progressed and they drank more wine their formal conversation began to wane and they looked bored enough to fall asleep.

I have no idea what Peter said in a lull in their conversation to indicate that he was from Australia — or perhaps it was just that we too were speaking English — but whatever it was, it catapulted Mr Hawke into action. Slim in his dark suit, elegant and handsome, he suddenly jumped to his feet and came across to our table. With a bow in my direction, he asked us to join them. No sooner were we seated than our glasses were refilled with Swiss white wine and he jumped once again to his feet, bowed again in my direction, and asked me to dance.

No one else was dancing. There was no dance floor. I had never seen anyone dance there before. There was no dance music, just the clompy Swiss mountain music playing in the background. But, delighted at the unexpected turn of events, I rose to my feet, smiling, and we sailed off among the tables.

I wish I could remember what we talked about while we danced — I think the scent of his aftershave must have gone to my head and destroyed my memory. I do remember admiring his thick wavy grey hair from close up. He was an excellent dancer and we put on a terrific performance. Then he led me back to our table, drew out my chair and bowed again. For a moment I thought he was going to kiss my hand. He was so debonair that I was completely bedazzled. I smiled and thanked him — I would have been in favour of a repeat performance — but Peter instantly decided it was time to leave.

\* \* \*

Each time Peter came to Geneva it was harder to say goodbye than before and the transition to our other worlds more difficult. He once sent me a tape of love poems which he read in a quiet, tender voice; I especially remember a heart-string-tugging one about pebbles and sand warm in one's hand in the sunshine. He wrote or telephoned every day. Occasionally there would be a gap of a few days and then I would receive a bundle of five or six aerograms all at once. We both spent many hours writing to tell each another every detail of our daily lives.

Until a time came when there was nothing. No letters, no telephone calls, not even a postcard. I felt as if I had been cut in half and only one half of me had survived. Whatever could have happened? With each empty day I felt more desperate and imagined a greater calamity. Australia had never seemed so far away. Perhaps a car accident. A heart attack. Some kind of natural disaster — surely whatever it was would have to be very serious to prevent him from getting in touch somehow. I searched in vain in Geneva for an Australian newspaper in case there'd been an earthquake or a tidal wave over Melbourne but the only mention of Australia I was able to find was in the *New York Herald Tribune* which reported: 'Mouse Plague Downunder'. For the life of me I could not see how mice could prevent a telecommunications expert from communicating with Geneva.

It wasn't until several weeks later that I learnt that he had been travelling all over the country with a team of satellite experts installing a state-of-the-art satellite communications system involving geostationary orbits. All that communications expertise and no way of contacting me.

Ten frantic days went by with no news. I kept posting Swiss aerograms and receiving nothing in return. Then one night the strident shrill of the telephone awoke me. The voice I longed to hear said: 'It's me. I'm calling from Canberra.'

Fighting back the sudden onrush of tears of relief so they wouldn't spoil this precious moment I gulped and said:

'Thank heavens you've phoned! I've been so worried. I've been calling and calling you and writing too. We need to talk: I think I'm pregnant. What shall we do?'

Peter muttered something unintelligible at the other end. Perhaps there was something wrong with the line and he hadn't heard what I said. I repeated it in a louder, clearer voice, stressing each word and then added plaintively: 'I've been feeling sick and my period is late.'

Suddenly a strange, unknown, authoritative male voice came on the line. 'This is a demonstration call over the new satellite communication system,' it intoned to my horror. 'We have given our international expert the honour of inaugurating the system and he has chosen to call your number in Switzerland. This conversation is being broadcast worldwide by satellite …'

As it happened, it was a false alarm. I wasn't pregnant after all.

Next time Peter came to Geneva we spent our evening hours discussing whether he should take premature retirement and come to live in Switzerland permanently or whether I should move to Australia. Whichever we decided, one of us would have to give up family, friends, home and career to move to the other side of the world. In the end I agreed that it would be more difficult for him to live in a French-speaking environment than for me to live where English was spoken. Also, he had little hope of finding a job in Geneva at the age of fifty-four whereas it didn't really matter where I lived, I would always be offered simultaneous interpreting work at international conferences once I had made known my new address. So, in the end we decided I would start by moving to Australia for a trial period of six months and if I liked it I would alternate, living six months in each hemisphere for a few years. The cost of living was so much lower in Australia than in Switzerland that I could easily earn enough during my six months in Geneva to provide for myself generously during my time in the Antipodes if no interpreting work was at first forthcoming — it would probably take a few years to make known my new professional domicile to all concerned.

After Peter had left, I spent many sleepless nights wondering whether this was the right decision. I had travelled to so many countries in my professional life; I knew I could settle down and be happy in almost any of them. But I would miss so much if I went to live on the other side of the world in an Anglo-Saxon country where everything was so different: their way of thinking, the food, the culture and the lifestyle — where not only was English considered superior to other languages, even beautiful languages like Italian, French, Spanish and Russian, but there were no bidets in the bathrooms and no shutters at the windows, just flimsy curtains so the daylight could come in and wake you at dawn? Where cakes, biscuits and croissants were big, clumsy and too sweet instead of small and dainty, crisp and delicate? In fact, it seemed to me that all Australians had an enormous sweet tooth. I remember when Great Britain applied to join the Common Market and I sat between the two Prime Ministers, interpreting for them, each of them whispering negative comments in my ear because they each thought I was from their country and therefore on their side!

And the Working Group when France insisted that tinned baked beans be listed under jam rather than vegetables because of their high sugar content.

I would miss Africa too; it would be too far away for me to expect conference offers there. No more visits to Africa, how could I live happily without a spell in Africa every now and then?

But in my heart of hearts, I knew I had already decided. I couldn't imagine life without Peter. It had to be Australia in the end.

I wallowed in misery for a few nights, thinking of all the things I would miss. I would be twenty-seven hours door-to-door away from my children. However, I knew they were settled and happy. Steffie was working in New York, Marc had become a successful business executive and Cassie was at Madrid University — from time to time I had been flying over to Madrid to spend a weekend with her and visit the art galleries. But she would soon finish her studies and return to Geneva — the School of Interpretation at Geneva University — where her father would keep an eye on her and I would send her a return air ticket to visit us in Australia during holidays.

The following day with gritted teeth I put a 'House to Let' advertisement up in the United Nations staff-room, half hoping no one would answer. I asked for what I thought was a rather high rent to discourage would-be tenants because I could hardly bear the thought of strangers sitting in my garden, looking at my view of the lake and the Mont Blanc, perhaps smoking in the house and filling my curtains with the smell of cigarettes. Supposing they chopped down my cherry trees or their dog damaged my beautiful deep-red velvety rambling rose on the trellis outside the kitchen window or the three apricot trees *en espalier* against the garage wall?

    I received a dozen or so calls in answer to my advertisement and finally chose a diplomat from South America because he and his family would at least play the sort of music my house was used to.

✳ ✳ ✳

At the end of the conference we left for Australia together, stopping over in Singapore for two delightful days, staying at the old Raffles Hotel and making sure we had a gin sling in the Long Bar each evening. At the airport Duty-Free I bought a large bottle of my favourite Guerlain perfume: *L'Habit Rouge*. It was really a man's perfume; as I walked away, I thought how nice it would be to make love to a man smelling of it so I went back and bought another bottle for Peter.

✳ ✳ ✳

# PART 2
# MELBOURNE

While searching for a house, we stayed at the George Powlett in East Melbourne, where we had been before. One of the first things I did was to go to the Hill of Content bookshop at the top of Bourke Street where, with the help of the friendly man working there, I chose ten books by Australian authors about Australia. I started with Patrick White, Christina Stead and Thomas Keneally. I declined a copy of *Strine* — it would have been my umpteenth — just about everyone had given me one. Besides, *Strine* was not something I enjoyed — in fact, I disliked it intensely.

The second thing on my list was to telephone Lady Anne Kerr who lived in Sydney. Colleagues in Paris and Geneva had entrusted me with various messages for her; they had worked with her before her marriage in 1975 when she was Anne Robson, French-English simultaneous interpreter and an active member of our professional association. She and Sir John lived in a Quarterdeck apartment in Kirribilli. They invited me for sherry that evening and as I was leaving she made me promise to visit them each time I went to Sydney. I did, and many times; we drank a lot of sherry and caught up with news of colleagues, interpreters and diplomats we knew. Sir John generally joined us, relaxing in his favourite armchair, but participated very little in our conversation. Interpreters can speak very fast, and once the other person has said half a sentence, an interpreter knows what the other half will be, so our exchanges can be rapid and difficult to intercept. I'm afraid in normal life people find us impolite because we rarely wait for other people to finish their sentences before we cut in —that is just one of the drawbacks of our profession.

Anne was working on her book *Lanterns over Pinchgut*. Later, she sent me a copy of the draft to read and asked for my comments. I enjoyed reading it, especially the parts relating to her life as an interpreter at the first international conferences held in Australia. The book was finally published in 1988 by Macmillan. Later, when I lived in Australia, I visited her often. To be able to talk about our profession was a rare link with the European interpreting scene which we both missed enormously.

Anne was greatly amused by my story about the US Congressman who, in 1988, when testifying at the Joint National Committee on Languages, maintained that it was not necessary to waste money teaching foreign languages in American schools, concluding:

'*If English was good enough for Jesus Christ, it's good enough for me.*'

※ ※ ※

Peter and I finally found a charming, white-washed fisherman's cottage in Brighton, five minutes from the sea. The owner lived next door and told us both houses were 150 years old. It made me think of a dolls' house: the rooms were so tiny we had to hunt for small furniture to fit. As neither of us were tall our new house suited us perfectly. The old timber mantelpiece came away from the wall if you put anything on it, the floors were not flat, the old-fashioned papered walls were not straight and the floorboards trembled when you walked on them. But there was a huge frangipani tree covered in blossom on one side of the front door and a beautifully scented pink standard rose on the other. The small gardens front and back had rich dark soil which proved very fertile. I was able to grow runner beans in neat rows and pick them while still small and tender, making the most delicious summer salads.

That first Christmas Cassie came to stay with us and we took her to Phillip Island. We were enjoying a picnic lunch on the beach when a freak wave suddenly swept over us, carrying off all our possessions: clothes, Peter's leather shoes, my camera and handbag. Fortunately, we were able to rush into the sea and retrieve everything. The problem now was our dripping wet clothes, and we had nothing dry to put on. As the sun began to set it turned quite cold. Peter calmly put all his clothes on wet in his stalwart Anglo-Saxon way, but Cassie and I made a spoilt European fuss. Peter tied my red skirt to the string of the kite he always kept in the boot of his car (you never knew when it might come in handy). He and Cassie then ran up and down the beach until my skirt was almost dry. That evening we shivered in our damp clothes as we watched koalas hiding in the trees and later by torchlight, fairy penguins coming out of the sea and making a dash for their burrows, surrounded by gasping tourists hunched up in the dark. Cassie, shivering in her damp bikini, was bemoaning the fact that all her other clothes were still too wet to wear.

※　※　※

At the bottom of our back garden was a wooden garage which also housed an outside toilet (fortunately there was also one inside the house) and a small laundry with a sink and a washing machine. Our garden backed on to Mrs Douglas' garden in a parallel street and sometimes we talked over the high wooden back fence. When walking past her house I had particularly admired her apricot trees, laden with fruit.

The Melbourne heat took me by surprise. I had never experienced such temperatures. In Switzerland summers were considered hot — especially when compared with English ones — and in Spain, where we often went on holiday, it was even hotter. However, I found a Melbourne summer temperature of 41, and even 43 degrees on one or two occasions, quite frightening. I experienced a feeling of panic when touching a door handle or knives and forks in the kitchen drawer, when they felt warm.

One morning after Peter had left for work, I went down to the laundry to do the weekly washing. I was perspiring and my clothes felt damp and sticky; the perspiration was trickling down my arms. On an impulse, I took all my clothes off and put them in the washing machine with the rest. There was no one to see and Cassie was still asleep indoors.

I could hear Mrs Douglas in her garden on the other side of the high wooden fence. Suddenly, she called out: 'Hallo, there. Would you like some apricots?'

Now there is a strange thing about being in the nude: it seems difficult to talk normally as one does when dressed. I found it impossible to hold a chatty conversation with Mrs Douglas while standing there naked. Perhaps I should have said: 'Just a minute. I'm naked. I'll go inside and put some clothes on.' But how could I confess to being naked in the garage? A voice inside me said: 'She'll think you're crazy, or that you have strange daytime activities. Why tell her? She doesn't need to know. It's all right, she can't see you.'

But I just couldn't bring myself to say a word. I felt guilty, as if caught in the act of doing something shameful. I was too embarrassed to speak. I knew I was guilty. The remnants of a Protestant streak going back to my British ancestors lurked in the depths of my soul.

Suddenly an irrepressible urge to giggle overtook me. I tried to fight it but knew I couldn't trust myself to speak.

I put a firm hand over my mouth but I was bursting with laughter and strange bubbly noises emerged nevertheless. I was terrified Mrs Douglas would hear me laughing and think I had suddenly become insane.

'Hallo! I know you're there. Why don't you answer me?' Mrs Douglas repeated.

I struggled again with the giggles but I just could not control them.

All I wanted was to dash back into the house and put some clothes on so that I could talk to her normally.

Torn between the wish to be polite to her, and the enormous guilt of talking to her in the nude, I am ashamed to say I pretended not to hear her and I tiptoed back into the house to get dressed. Later I sent Cassie round to say 'hallo' and she came back with a basket of beautiful ripe apricots. But in spite of all the years that have passed since then, the moment I think of kind Mrs Douglas and her delicious, ripe, juicy apricots, I am engulfed by a feeling of guilt, and a fit of the giggles.

The Dendy cinema in Brighton was showing a French film called *Love in the Grass*. Those who went expecting to see something titillating must have been disappointed, especially in view of the reputation the French seem to have in Australia. The film was in fact an innocent story of a boy and girl whose parents were killed during a bomb attack during World War II. The children crept out of the *débris*, stayed together and looked after one another. '*En herbe*' in French means 'budding,' for example a '*poète en herbe*' is a 'budding poet'. The film should have been called 'budding love' or something referring to a love story between children. Just another mistranslation to add to my secret pile ...

While Peter was at work one morning, Cassie and I went to the beach, but the moment we sat down a cloud of black flies appeared out of nowhere. They landed on our arms and backs and legs and even when we hit them whilst trying to chase them away, they seemed reluctant to move. We packed up our things and walked to the nearest pharmacy where we bought a tube of insect repellent cream. Then we sat down again and carefully covered ourselves with it. It certainly worked. The flies died instantly — on our skin. Soon we were both covered with dead flies. The only solution was to stay in the water. Sunbathing was obviously out of the question. It seemed Australian flies were different — they were a pioneering, persistent breed.

Then Cassie went back to Switzerland to school and left me without an ally in this strange new fly-blown country to face my first Australian barbecue. Unfortunately, we arrived rather late so the other guests had already been drinking for a while which may explain why, when I first walked in, our host walked straight up and kissed me on the lips. I managed to turn my head away in the nick of time and kissed him back on the cheek.

'What's wrong?' he asked. 'I thought French women were fast.'

Then he turned to Peter and said in a loud whisper: 'Nice tits.'

I blushed and felt very embarrassed. No European would make such a comment in front of everybody. They might look at you appraisingly, but no such words would pass their lips. I was out of my depth.

The evening had not started well. It got worse.

In the garden was a large trestle table surrounded by seated wives. The men stood in a group round the barbecue, beer in hand, laughing, telling jokes and slapping one another on the back as they bellowed with laughter. At first I sat politely with the women, nodding and smiling. Some of them smelt of a sickly-sweet perfume like toilet deodorant and many wore funny little old-fashioned rings with a minute diamond in the middle. The scraps of their conversation that I was able to understand in spite of their unusual vowels were of no interest to me whatsoever — one of them talked about chickenpox symptoms while another about a new washing powder she had discovered. I got up — as I would have done in Europe — and went to join the men who seemed to be having a much better time.

Everyone froze. It seemed the women thought I wanted to steal their husbands especially, as one of them explained to me later, since I was wearing French perfume, a silk scarf and earrings. The men felt they could not continue telling sexist or smutty jokes in the presence of a woman, an unknown one at that. I realised too late that Australia was different from Europe. Men and women did not mix at barbecues like they did at cocktail parties, where the first thing you had to do was circulate.

Fortunately, Peter immediately understood the situation and came to my rescue. He went over to the table and sat on my empty chair with the women. Soon he had them answering his questions (perhaps about chickenpox symptoms and washing powders?) and the ice was broken.

I believe Australia has changed a lot since those days.

Subsequently, we were invited to many barbecues and parties and I gradually learnt the rules. I also discovered that, when talking to a woman, Australian men rarely looked at her face. They directed their conversation entirely to her breasts. I began to notice the obsession Australian men had with women's 'boobs' as they called them — I had never heard that word before. So many jokes and much of their 'blokey' conversation referred to that part of a woman's anatomy. Television programmes corroborated my theory, so did magazines and newspapers. I felt this obsession must, somehow, be linked to the Protestant streak. I read somewhere that Anglo-Saxon babies were not breast fed for as long as European babies and were thus deprived of contact with their mothers' breasts. It all made sense when I remembered that in many European countries people joked in those days about babies being breastfed until they started school in Italy — in spite of the fact that they had teeth. In Switzerland people joked that baby boys were breastfed until they joined the Army — which was compulsory at eighteen in those days, at least for a week or two every year.

At an International Women's Conference in Denmark, at which I interpreted, the agenda item under discussion was 'The advantages of breastfeeding'. There had been a scandal the year before when out-of-date powdered milk had been sold in African countries supported by an enormous commercial publicity campaign giving African women the impression that powdered milk was pure and sterile and better for babies than breast milk. I well remember interpreting a buxom, extremely well-endowed Swiss delegate, doing her best to redress the situation, explaining that women should alternate left and right breasts at regular feeds throughout the day. I recall even more clearly the beautiful, slim, elegant lady from Ghana who rose proudly to her feet in her gracefully draped robes and elegant head-dress and explained that this was not possible in Africa, for a reason all African women knew only too well. The Danish President having expressed her lack of knowledge on this subject, the lady from Ghana then explained:

'In our countries, Madame President, only the right breast may be given to the infant. The left is reserved for its father.'

Strange, how different Australian men's obsession with women's breasts was from the preoccupations of French men. In Paris in the late 1940s, I recall that the young men I met through my future French husband never talked about girls' breasts. Rather they waxed lyrical about the charms and delights of the *'rivière parisienne'* (Parisian river). If a girl was walking towards you wearing trousers and you could see daylight between her thighs, she had a *'rivière parisienne'* — which seemed to be a big 'turn-on' for the young men of Paris in those days. No talk whatsoever of breasts. Different countries, different cultures … *Altri tempi!*

\* \* \*

Little by little I began to learn more about the Australian way of life. The omnipresent 'Protestant streak' was flourishing: the more unpleasant something was, the better it was for you. Anything pleasurable was decadent and therefore bad. Bread containing seeds that got stuck in your teeth was good for you. Protestant bread. You could buy creamy lathering soap in the supermarket with an acceptable perfume but that was indulgent, even rather sinful; it was much better to buy soap with hard bits in it that hurt your skin when you showered. Protestant soap. Luther and Calvin had a lot to answer for. The idea of putting a pebble in your shoe because it is so wonderful when you take it out, must have been invented by them too.

Another big difference I noticed between Australia and Europe, which may seem trivial but in fact is quite significant, is the way pedestrians behave at traffic lights.

If there are no cars coming in Paris or Geneva no one

would stop and wait because the traffic lights are red. In Australia I found it infuriating to have to wait for them to turn green quite needlessly. No doubt this too has something to do with Calvin and Luther? In Mediterranean countries rules are considered more as guidelines.

On the other hand, I was fascinated by the starry sky and the fact that the stars in Australia are so different from those one sees in Switzerland. The Southern Cross is so beautiful I have spent many hours studying the beautiful Australian night sky.

It was while we lived in Selwyn Street, Brighton, that I encountered the most handsome man I had ever met. One morning the doorbell rang and there he was. Tall, slim and tanned, with the body of a Greek god. He had broad shoulders, a small, tight bottom and long, slim legs. His hair was unruly, curly and brown, almost shoulder length; his sparkling brown eyes shone with a mischievous twinkle. I gasped when I saw him. I felt as though I were suddenly inside a fairy story and Prince Charming had arrived on my doorstep to carry me off on his white horse.

I suppose living in an unknown country was an adventure but on a day-to-day basis not knowing anyone apart from Peter meant I felt rather lonely when he wasn't there.

'I'm the gasman,' he explained. 'You telephoned? Your oven doesn't work properly?'

Our oven was as old as the house and I could never get it to do what I wanted.

I had always thought of gas-men as middle-aged, overweight, probably cockney — kindly souls, rather fatherly. Wearing baggy trousers and probably a cap. But this Australian gasman could have been a film star. Just looking at him in amazement made me forget what I should be saying or doing ...

I stammered: 'Yes, yes, I rang the Gas Company ...' and tried to collect my thoughts. He looked strong too. Those muscular arms, tanned and powerful, were surely not those of the average Australian gasman?

This was an amazing country indeed.

'Please come in,' I managed to whisper, leading him to the alcove in the kitchen wall where the old gas cooker stood, hoping there weren't too many cobwebs behind it, and wishing I had cleaned and polished it that morning.

He walked with ease but there was some shyness beneath his self-confidence.

Watching Spanish dancers in Málaga I had always been fascinated by their small round muscular bottoms, their tight-fitting black trousers like a second skin. This gasman's bottom was worthy of any flamenco dancer and his tight cyclamen jeans showed it off to advantage. He strode into our tiny kitchen, turned on the oven taps, placed a thermostat inside, clicked the timer on his watch and turned to me with a smile.

'We have fifteen minutes to wait while the oven heats up,' he said invitingly.

My mind raced. A few attractive possibilities flashed through my mind. Instead, I tried to look composed and suggested:

'Would you like a cup of coffee? I could make some ...'

My voice trailed away hesitatingly.

'That would be very nice,' he said firmly. 'May I sit down?'

These old kitchen chairs are not good enough I thought as I filled the kettle. They looked too small and rickety for this tall athletic figure.

'Tell me about yourself,' he proposed. 'We have plenty of time.'

'Well, I'm from Switzerland,' I began. 'I've been in Australia for about a month now. I fell in love with this pretty old cottage though it is very small and the floors aren't flat. Because the walls aren't straight the furniture always seems crooked. But it's ideal really, I'm only here for six months at a time. The rooms are so small they remind me of Mrs Tiggy-Winkle ...'

I paused to make the coffee, noticing guiltily that I had deliberately said 'I' instead of 'we'.

'The cooker is very old and so is the stone sink. It blocked up soon after I moved in and when I unscrewed the pipe underneath, I found this strange square silver spoon — it looks like an antique. What do you think?'

I couldn't stop myself from saying 'I moved in' and 'I unscrewed' though I knew perfectly well I was totally incapable of unscrewing anything and I should have said 'Peter unscrewed'.

The spoon was unusual and a little bent. After examining it we drank our coffee.

'Well, the fifteen minutes are up. I'd better have another look at the oven.'

He rose to his feet and started turning the taps on the stove.

I turned my back on him as I washed the cups, relieved that I had behaved in true British style. For once I hadn't blushed. At least I didn't think so ...

'There we are,' he said 'I've adjusted the taps. Tightened them up a bit so now we'll have another try. Another fifteen minutes to wait. What shall we do this time?'

I hoped my face hadn't gone scarlet. In a firm voice I answered:

'Now it's your turn. Tell me about yourself and I'll make another cup of coffee.'

'Well, I haven't been in this job long. I'm really a surfer. I've been surfing since I was a kid. I ran away from home as a teenager to do my own thing. Until now I've lived on the beach, surfing all day, sleeping at night on the beach. It's never very cold here, you don't need many clothes and the dole is ample for food and a few beers. It's a beaut life! Travelling around all the time, moving as the weather changes, to stay where it's sunny. But now I've met a girl and we want to get married, so I have to earn some money ...'

Wonderful Australia! Real people, not human ants, working without lifting their heads to look at the world around them. Most people I knew in Europe lived to work;

work was their life. They hardly had any time or energy left to think about anything else. No time to smell a rose or watch a bird on the wing. But here was a wise man who worked to live and do the things he wanted.

Unfortunately, the oven worked perfectly from that day on.

\*　\*　\*

Curiously, when in Australia I am considered a 'pommy,' while in Geneva and England people comment on my Australian accent. Yes, I am Australian. Yes, I am British and Swiss. And French. Definitely Spanish, especially when I am speaking Spanish, and Russian when I am speaking Russian. I belong to the world, not to one country.

Perhaps if everyone learnt another language or two they might feel the same, and maybe then there would be less conflict in the world.

\*　\*　\*

One day passing through Sydney, I found myself in the vicinity of Central Quay. I heard an amazing sound and, following its direction, came across a young man of about thirty, bearded and extremely thin, dressed in jeans and an old rather tattered tee-shirt, sitting against a wall in the sun, surrounded by a crowd of onlookers. He was playing the didgeridoo and had an open attaché case in front of him already half full of coins and a few notes. Sitting in the lotus position he held a stick between one foot and the other knee and with one hand he was banging a rhythm on it with a second stick. The didgeridoo was like a large tube, wider at the far end and from it came the most amazing sounds, a captivating rhythm and spellbinding vibrations. The rhythm accelerated and became more intricate, his neck muscles began to tense, his nose started twitching and as he played, his nostrils opened and closed — soon his knees were beating the rhythm too and then his whole body. It was a confronting and all-engulfing experience.

A tidy, no-nonsense lady who could be a discreet chambermaid from a nearby hotel or a theatre dresser, I thought, was tightly clutching her homemade canvas handbag. With her hair neatly tucked into a snug white beret she looked as though she would be impervious to music. But as I watched, she started to sway very gently and then finally, to move from one neat foot to the other in rhythm with the beat.

Some passing children threw a handful of coins onto the folded newspaper in the bottom of the open case. Then two plump little girls, one fair with blue eyes and the other dark, walked hand in hand in front of the crowd and carefully placed their offerings in the case, stepping over the player's feet and then back to their smiling mother.

It was all I could do to stop myself from breaking into a dance with the rhythm, letting go of my political correctness and just enjoying the beat, but the aboriginal world was unknown to me and full of mystery. I had no idea where dancing on my own in front of a crowd of onlookers might lead, and it was certainly not the right thing for a United Nations simultaneous interpreter to do.

The vibrations of the didgeridoo affected my whole body in a strange, primitive way and took me back to Africa, to Senegal or the Congo, or to Poto-Poto when, on Sunday afternoons in the shade of the trees, drums would play and people would dance to a similar irresistible beat.

I felt very grateful to the slim young musician who had drawn me back to the very origins of music. I hoped he understood how I felt. Surely, if he could play such deeply meaningful music he would be able to sense my gratitude.

PART 3

# CANBERRA

The government department Peter worked for moved to Canberra and therefore, so did we. We rented a pretty little house in Page, five minutes' walk from the post office. It was much colder in Canberra, and at first I was puzzled by the fact that the toilet window in our house (and everywhere else we went) could not be closed completely. About one third of it remained open, with just the flyscreen to keep out the cold. When I enquired of the tall dragon-lady who came from time to time to inspect our house and garden, and make sure we were taking good care of everything, she explained that it was 'for health reasons — to let in the fresh air'. That was fine in the hot weather, but what about winter when it was cold outside? I complained to everyone — I'm afraid I do not belong to the 'suffering is good for you' brigade. Someone told me that Dick Smith sold heated toilet seats, which was at least a step in the right direction. At long last I had found someone — this wonderful man, Dick Smith — who, like me, needed to feel warm and comfortable to produce results. I managed to procure one of his catalogues and there it was. Triumphantly I telephoned to order one to be delivered urgently, but in spite of the many telephone calls and trips to his shops in various places, the answer was always 'No Longer Available'. The Protestant streak had won in the end.

Peter's office was in Belconnen; there were five or six tall office buildings, each painted a different colour: Peter's was green. Like most of his colleagues, he cycled to work each morning with his umbrella and document case on the back of his bicycle, behind the saddle. They all had impressive-looking document cases, which you'd think contained important international records, minutes of secret meetings, official archives or journals. However, they just contained their sandwiches for lunch. For some reason, when I saw the public servants pedalling their way to work in the mornings, I thought of Jacques Tati or Mr Bean. From all over Canberra they pedalled madly in the direction of Belconnen, like a coven of witches on their broomsticks.

Sometimes, Peter would have to catch the first flight to Sydney or Melbourne for a meeting. Our alarm would ring early, bringing us brutally out of a deep, satisfied sleep. 'I'll just have five more minutes' he would say, turning off the alarm.

'That's dangerous,' I would mumble sleepily. I couldn't say anymore because he was kissing me, his arms and legs wrapping round me gently, while I rubbed his back and he groaned with pleasure. We kissed as if our lips would be impossible to separate, impossible to tell which were his and which were mine.

Then suddenly he would bound out of bed, into the cold, dark, Canberra 6 o'clock morning and the shower. I reluctantly donned my dressing gown, and, eyes still half closed, dragged my slippered feet into the kitchen towards breakfast.

Soon the kettle was on, the toast toasting and somehow I found myself in the bathroom when he stepped, dripping, out of the shower. We kissed again and he drank me like a thirsty man in the desert would gulp down the milk from of a heaven-sent coconut.

I sat shivering in my dressing-gown, trying not to show I was cold, while he drank his tea and finished his breakfast. 'I brought these for you to eat on the way' — I fished out of the cupboard a packet of Mars Bars for him to take.

We kissed again. His skin was freshly shaven and soft, so soft to kiss and rub my face against.

Then he carried his things out to the car and I heard the engine start up as I settled back into bed and sank down into the pillow.

For the next five years, as planned, I lived six months in Canberra, followed by six months in Geneva — Australian spring and summer, followed by Swiss spring and summer. At each end, the lilac trees were just beginning to bloom in the garden.

Each June I arrived in Geneva in time for the International Labour Conference where Bob Hawke must have heard my voice in his headphones quite often — I wondered whether he recognised my budding ('*en herbe!*') Australian accent.

Peter came to Geneva for the last few weeks whenever he could, and we left just as the *vendanges* (wine-harvest) finished, having taken part in all the festivities, sampled the new white wine in all the Swiss villages roundabout and danced to the music of the local musicians in traditional costume. Then we flew back to our little house in Canberra where spring was just beginning, the lilac trees near the fishpond were preparing to bloom, and the Australian conference season was just starting.

Gradually I got to know this country of beautiful land- and seascapes, where the trees looked like flower arrangements and surrounding Canberra the sheep were earth-coloured instead of white. There were flocks of pink galahs in the sky, and sometimes the trees were full of multicoloured lorikeets like flowers that suddenly rose from the trees and flew away in a colourful cloud. A land of technicolour sunsets and enchanted flowers, birds and animals worthy of Lewis Carroll.

It was a while before my new professional domicile became known which meant that at first, I had little work. As I watched my public servant partner ride off to Belconnen on his bicycle in true Australian style, I wondered how I would fill my day. The radio programmes all seemed to be about sport; on all frequencies someone was kicking a ball about somewhere or hitting it with something or other. Until one wonderful morning I discovered the Classic FM radio station and my life changed for the better: suddenly Australia became much more attractive. I tuned all our radios to that station and music played wherever I went in the house. It was like wallpaper in all the rooms.

One morning my attention was caught by the words 'Salle Pleyel in Paris'. I pricked up my ears. The presenter was introducing a concert live from Paris — the music was by an Australian composer. Then the composer himself started to speak in halting 'school-boy French'.

He was doing his best but it was a struggle. 'Oh dear,' I thought. 'He'd have done better to speak in English with or without an interpreter or not to speak at all.' Then I heard the word 'Coo-ee'. He was explaining that it was typically Australian, first used by Aborigines and later copied by settlers, calling out to one another in the bush. He sounded so sincere, so earnest and I cringed with embarrassment on his behalf. He must have been baffled by the awkward silence that followed his words. I could imagine the horror on the faces of the Parisian audience. They were having trouble believing their ears. *Couilles*, pronounced 'coo-eey,' is a French word commonly used for 'testicles'. You often hear: 'So-and-so doesn't have the *couilles* to tell his boss he wants a raise' or 'Henri doesn't have the *couilles* to tell his wife she needs cookery lessons.'

It must have been quite a challenge to sit back and listen to music written about 'all-important in Australia' testicles ... Imagining Australians calling out to one another in the bush 'Balls' and the reply coming back through the trees: 'Balls' ...

I wondered whether anyone would have the *couilles* to explain to the composer the significance of what he had said ...

Peter's work colleagues' wives were very friendly and invited me out one morning a few days after our arrival. They called it 'morning tea' but actually everyone drank coffee. Once we were all assembled in the café, my hostess stood me in front of an array of delicious cakes in a glass case and said: 'I'll shout.' This intrigued me considerably. Why would she shout, to whom and what about? In the end I put it down to an unknown Australian custom, perhaps something to do with the traditional owners of the country. I hoped she wouldn't shout 'Coo-ee'…

As it happened, she didn't shout at all, as she was very well-behaved and spoke quite softly. She told me she had been busy planting sweet-pea seeds for spring. After buying the very best and planting them carefully she was just about to water them when the words of a gardening expert came back to her: 'They'll need some lime in your sort of soil.'

Where could she find lime? Her husband had mixed some cement last weekend, she remembered, and had said something about lime. There was a bag of cement in the shed but no lime. 'Oh, well,' she thought. 'Cement probably contains lime.' She carefully sprinkled cement over the soil where she had planted the sweet-pea seeds. In her enthusiasm she then sprinkled a second handful and a third, seeing in her mind's eye the beautiful array of sweet peas that would result: large, healthy flowers of all colours.

It wasn't until she had finished watering the flowerbed that she realised the sweet-pea seeds were now set in concrete for ever.

I joined a choir days later and the three sopranos sitting next to me invited me to join them for a drink at the local club after singing practice one evening, to celebrate one of their birthdays. As we trooped into the crowded bar, Kaye turned around and called out to me at the top of her voice: 'Have you ever had an orgasm?'

I was shocked. Should I tell the truth? Australian women were full of surprises. There were a few minutes' silence while I tried to decide what to reply. I can't remember now what I did say in the end. Eventually I discovered what an orgasm was: a sickly pink cocktail, served in a cocktail glass the shape of Marie-Antoinette's breast, with a cherry on a toothpick.

I began to learn many new expressions and fell in love with 'journo' for journalist, 'milko' for milkman and 'garbo' for the rubbish collector.. I suppose one could hardly say 'rubbish-o' so, for once, I forgave them for using an American expression. People had a 'smoko' outside. Somebody said you couldn't print something or other 'for defo reasons' which puzzled me for a few minutes but once I understood I fell in love with that expression as well.

I also learnt about Germaine Greer and her books, which I hastened to read.

'Behind every successful man is a wife who cooks, cleans,

washes and sends him off to work in a clean shirt every morning' I read in a women's magazine. 'Yes,' I thought. 'And who welcomes him home every evening to a clean house and a tasty meal ready on the table.' Life was unfair. Why couldn't I too have a wife as well as a husband? Having a husband was fine, he changed the light bulbs, put out the rubbish bin and did odd jobs around the house and garden, as well as being nice to cuddle up to in bed at night. Having a wife as well would be even better: she could sleep downstairs, do the cleaning, shopping, cooking and make the odd cup of tea or coffee now and then, while I sat and read the paper or watched television. It is unfair that men should be so privileged.

\* \* \*

I was invited by the Russian department of the ANU (Australian National University) on several occasions to speak to the students about careers in translation and interpretation at United Nations and elsewhere. I met several interesting people there, including Rosh Ireland and Robert Dessaix.

Well, too, do I remember Gus' café in Bunda Street, now called 'Gus' Place'. We often went there because of its European ambiance, which made me feel at home. We became good friends with Gus but I deplored the fact that, in those days, there were no tables outside. 'Not allowed,' Gus explained. 'Too many flies. Not allowed by the Health

Authorities.' We must have improved our fly status over the following years because the Australian fly doesn't seem to intimidate us now as it did in the past; we were delighted when tables were at last allowed outside on the pavement. But I was still not satisfied. 'What we need now,' I told Gus, 'is a violinist, playing as he wanders between the tables.' But that wish was never fulfilled — at least, not as long as I lived in Canberra.

Many years later, after we had moved to Ulladulla on the South Coast, Gus opened a café here, too, but unfortunately it was not sufficiently profitable and did not last long.

\* \* \*

After a while a few conferences began to come my way. All the United Nations organisations I had worked for when domiciled in Geneva now recruited me whenever they had a conference in the Asia-Pacific or Oceania region. In this way they had to bring one less simultaneous interpreter out from Europe, making a considerable saving in their budget. Then they began asking me to recruit all the other interpreters locally as well.

My first Australian assignment in Canberra was the Fifth South Pacific Judicial Conference, held at the High Court in May 1982. Some days before it began I was instructed to call in to be briefed by the Marshall of the High Court, but he 'could not let me have any documents to study beforehand because they were too confidential.' The only paper I was allowed to see beforehand was the List of Participants, which meant nothing to me: The Rt. Hon. Sir this and the Hon. Sir that, The Hon. Mr Justice So-and-so, etc. Fortunately, I chose to wear a skirt that first day; there was quite a kerfuffle going on in the main hall when I arrived: one of the judges had refused to allow a female barrister to speak in court because she was wearing a trouser suit. I found it a most elegant trouser suit and very much like one of mine I could well have put on that morning. I heard the elderly, rather obese, judge threaten to go home and change into a skirt. A voice inside my head said: 'If only he would! What a sight that would be!' An excited crowd had gathered at the entrance to the courtroom; the case was finally postponed until the following day to allow the barrister concerned to go home and change into a skirt.

I had been instructed to use the special entrance at the back of the building where the judges' lift would take me straight to the top floor and the judges' quarters. Only two languages would be used at the conference: French and English; I was to interpret for the Chief Justice of Nouméa, New Caledonia, and the First President of the Court of Appeal of Papeete, French Polynesia. The night before the big day I was unable to sleep: my brain was in overdrive, trying to work out how I should address all those important people. I knew what I should say in England, the United States or at the United Nations but I had never had any dealing with judges in Australia. 'Your Worship' was for Mayors — should I call the Judges 'Your Honour'? I knew so few people in Australia — there was no one I could ask for advice. Would 'Sir' be enough in informal conversation? When did one say 'My Lord' or 'his Lordship'? The day before the conference I telephoned a few of Peter's colleagues' wives but no one had any idea.

So, as I stepped out of the lift on the top floor that first morning on the dot of 9 o'clock, I resigned myself to smiling and saying nothing until someone gave me a clue.

A giant of a man stepped forward to greet me, enormous hand outstretched. 'My name's Sid,' he said. 'You must be our interpreter. We need you desperately over here.' Then, after a glance at my name label on my jacket lapel: 'All right if I call you 'Val'? This is Les and Dick,' and he proceeded to introduce me to everyone. Unfortunately I never knew what their surnames were or how they fitted into the List of Participants, the only conference document I had been given.

It was an exhilarating week. The opening ceremony was impressive, starting with a concert by the RMS Duntroon brass band, dressed in red and gold. Throughout the conference we had coffee breaks on the roof and admired the glass pyramid, which someone smilingly explained was to enable overwrought judges to regain their composure. By sitting in its centre and linking up with cosmic forces, they would get their serenity and wisdom back. I made friends with many of them. Over coffee and biscuits we compared legal systems in different countries of the world, they tried out their school French on me and I corrected their grammar. I got to know 'my' judges from Nouméa and Papeete very well because I sat between them all day and at lunch and dinner in case they wished to converse with any English-speaking colleagues, as well as being at their side for the same reason at cocktail parties and other receptions in the evenings. French people are very formal, so I knew how to address them — one used the official title most of the time or 'monsieur' informally.

I did recognise Justice Lionel Murphy — I had seen him on television and his fruity voice was unmistakable and captivated me immediately. He was fatherly, gentle and kind and appreciated my efforts. He put an arm round my shoulders and sympathised, saying how hard it must be to go continually from one language into another, though I explained it really wasn't hard at all, just a knack. The Honourable Elizabeth Evatt told me about her experiences in the family court from a woman's point of view — we both felt we were in a man's world. We exchanged cards and agreed to keep in contact. But, in spite of all the friendly words we exchanged as we said goodbye, we lost touch after the conference.

And I still don't know how I should have addressed them or what the official titles or even the surnames were of 'Sid,' 'Mike,' 'Les,' 'Bill' and 'John' …

\* \* \*

The first time I worked for Imelda Marcos was at the Eighth World Congress of Anaesthesiology; we were interpreting for six thousand anaesthesiologists in the brand-new Convention Centre Imelda Marcos had had built in Metro Manila.

One afternoon, she hosted a *merienda* in the Malacañan Palace, to which she invited the Heads of Delegations and their wives. In old Spain, the merienda was a sort of afternoon high tea with all sorts of delicacies, including cold meats, sausages and egg dishes as well as cakes, biscuits, wine and coffee. A famous French lady doctor was invited as well as other non-English speaking eminent persons in the medical field, so Mrs Marcos asked for an interpreter to stand beside her as she shook everyone's hand upon arrival, to interpret any exchange of courtesies that might take place. I was that interpreter.

I remember Imelda wore such a thick layer of make-up that an irreverent little voice inside my head whispered that if she sneezed or laughed too violently, her face might fall off and lie on the floor like a mask. Having been a beauty queen in one's youth must leave one with an enormous responsibility.

'*Filipinos want beauty. I have to look beautiful so that poor Filipinos will have a star to look at from their slums,*' was one of her sayings.

There were about 250 guests queuing up to greet their hostess; I did what was expected of me. Mrs Marcos' make-up smiled at each guest and at me, but was she really smiling behind it?

Then we all filed into the main hall of the palace and I became a guest like everyone else. The hall was remarkable for its size and height and the fact that its walls were panelled with the most beautiful dark wood carvings and bas-reliefs. Everything was polished to perfection; there were larger-than-life carved figures, rural scenes, animals, plants and trees all round us. The ceiling too had beautiful carved panels of figures surrounding centrepieces with enormous sparkling candelabras. Tapestries decorated the high walls as well as red and gold silk draperies.

Round tables for eight had been set with handmade lace tablecloths, matching napkins and delicate china; at each place was a beautifully printed name-card and a small vase with a pale rose. Each lady also had a delicate handmade lace fan, with 'Imelda' embroidered on it. There was a photograph of Imelda Marcos on each plate and a printed copy of the keynote address she had delivered at the Congress opening.

In front of us, at the far end of the hall, was a dais with the head table, decorated with white flowers. Imelda stood there, bejewelled and smiling, with the President and Vice-Presidents of the Congress on either side.

Ferdinand was wheeled on and off in a contraption rather like a wheelchair except that, instead of being seated, he was standing. He smiled and waved; everyone clapped. Then he disappeared and we didn't see him again.

Imelda sat down and so did we.

A brigade of doormen in gold-braided uniform entered the room, closed the enormous, heavy carved doors and stood in front of them, two per doorway, as if on guard.

The guests started making polite conversation with their

neighbours as the waiters, in immaculate white with gold braid on their shoulders, served us with one dish of lavish food after another and a variety of drinks.

At about half past five Imelda Marcos rose to announce that the entertainment would now begin. I glanced at my watch because I had convened a meeting of all the conference interpreters at the close of work at the conference, that is to say at 6 o'clock, back in the Convention Centre in Metro Manila. I guessed it must have taken us about half an hour to drive to the palace from there, so it was about time I found out where I could get a taxi to take me back.

The entertainment turned out to be a concert; it was no longer polite to eat or drink, however tempting the food remaining on your plate might be.

A rather chubby girl of about ten came up on to the dais and started to sing, accompanied by an elderly rather obese gentleman on the piano. She had the same hairstyle as Shirley Temple and wore a similar dress, but unfortunately her singing voice was not as good as Shirley's and, what is more, she was slightly out of tune. She sounded very nervous. We all clapped politely, however, and before I could call over a waiter, a little boy of roughly the same age took her place. Then a group of three little girls came on stage and sang off key, followed by a small boy of about five who performed a violin solo. Then came a larger violinist who did his best.

A series of Shirley Temples of all shapes and sizes followed, with ribbons and bows in their hair and on their frilly dresses and male equivalents: well-scrubbed boys of all shapes and sizes in short or long trousers, stiff white shirts and bow ties, their hair partings immaculate. No butter could ever dream of melting in those pure little pink mouths. Some sang, some played the piano, the violin, the flute, or the guitar — many slightly off key. Not a lot. Just enough to make you wince. I found the violin performances particularly excruciating.

I began to get impatient. What would the interpreters think? They had probably all arrived in the interpreters' room by now and I was not there to greet them.

I finally succeeding in attracting the attention of one of the waiters but when I asked for the way out and could he call me a taxi, he looked horrified.

'No one may rise until Madam Marcos gives the signal,' he declared in a formal voice.

The child pianist on stage dropped his music on the floor and kept playing the beginning of the piece because that was all he could remember.

I thought I had finished with this sort of torture when my children grew up and it was no longer my duty to attend school concerts.

I could take no more. I rose to my feet. General consternation. Three waiters appeared from nowhere and gently pushed me back into my seat, explaining patiently once more that I could not stand until Madam Marcos rose to her feet.

I had attracted enough attention as it was, I thought, so I might as well make the most of it. Picking up my handbag, I made a dash to the only open door I could see, which was the one leading to the kitchen. All around me, people gasped — the waiters looked aghast as though what I had done might cost them their jobs. Once in the kitchen, I was surrounded by waiters and an urgent whispered conference took place in Tagalog. What should they do with me? I could hardly go back now and cause more disruption. Clearly, I could not stay in the kitchen where the chefs and waiters were hurrying about their work and I would be in their way. An older man standing back from the others seemed to be in charge so I went across to him and asked if he would help me order a taxi.

'Impossible,' he replied.

'Then please will you help me get out of the palace?' I asked.

I hoped Imelda Marcos thought I had been taken ill, or desperately needed the bathroom.

The kitchen staff were organised as in old Spain, where hierarchy was very important. The waiters were at the top — they dealt with the food. Then there were little boys at a lower level who dealt with the dirty dishes. The rather superior, dignified, elderly man in charge called over the smallest of the dirty-dishes boys and told him what to do in Tagalog. Nobody else moved. The child knew only a few words in English.

'Come,' he whispered, looking at me with awe as though I had committed a dreadful crime and he feared what I might do next.

'Follow!'

And I did.

Down a spiral staircase, through some empty basement rooms and then down a ramp into a damp tunnel.

The boy was obviously ill at ease. He almost ran. I followed as fast as I could in my high-heeled cocktail shoes. It was a long, dark, damp way. For more than ten minutes we hurried along the tunnel in semi-darkness; I noticed along both sides of the tunnel piles of large boxes and chests and packing cases. Was it a storing place for unwanted artworks? Or?

Perhaps my imagination was running away with me, but I couldn't help being reminded of a trip to Alexandria many years before, when I had been shown King Farouk's Palace and, underneath, his escape tunnel to the sea where a boat was always waiting. Along either side were statuettes, silverware, boxes of precious jewellery, candelabras, framed paintings ...

No, I must have been dreaming. The drama of the 'get away' must have been playing games with my mind.

A patch of daylight finally appeared in the distance. I was out of breath and the heel had come off one of my shoes. It was an enormous relief to see the patch of light grow bigger and brighter until I could see trees and grass in the sunshine. The small boy touched his forehead and bowed slightly, then turned and ran back as fast as he could.

I found myself alone on a country road. Not a building, not a soul in sight. I waited there in the sunshine, getting more and more impatient until finally a car appeared. I stepped out to stop it and the driver kindly took me back into town where I was able to catch a taxi to the Convention Centre and my interpreters' meeting. Nobody would have believed my story so I didn't waste time telling it.

'Sorry I'm late,' was all I said.

My hurried departure from her merienda cannot have upset Imelda too much because a few months later she asked me to create a Conference Interpreting School to be attached to the new Convention Centre. I was wondering how I should respond to this request when she asked me to go and discuss it with her.

When I learnt that she required all languages to go through Tagalog, my answer became clear.

However, I did continue to work quite often in Manila in the years that followed and fell in love with the old, walled part of town, Intramuros, with its old churches and the cathedral, the cool shady cloisters and courtyards with flowers and fountains playing, its cobblestone-paved streets, cafés and restaurants, old houses with wrought iron balconies, guitars playing, cool shady museums. It was full of the atmosphere of old Spanish colonial times, all so peaceful and soothing.

I remember, too, interpreting in the English booth in 1986 when Corazon Aquino had taken Imelda's place. It was another large conference with several thousand delegates. Standing in the interpretation booth on high, I looked down as Corazon arrived, deliberately five minutes late. A small, modest figure, dressed in yellow. The moment she entered the auditorium, everyone rose to their feet and started to applaud. The emotion in the hall was palpable. The applause lasted several minutes; many had tears on their faces. People Power had won the day and martial law had been replaced by normality, in the hands of this earnest little woman who had nothing in common with a beauty queen.

It was in Manila that I tasted my first mango. I had never come across them in Switzerland. I found them exotic and quite delicious; each time I worked in the Philippines from then on, my lunch consisted of three or four mangoes. I walked to the market on my way to work in the morning, where a bought three or four and a newspaper. Then, at lunchtime, when everyone else went off to a restaurant, I stayed behind in the booth, spread out the newspaper and managed somehow to cut them in half with the miniature nail scissors I kept in my handbag.

Only one person discovered my secret. One day, the delegate from Dahomey came back early from lunch and found me, wallowing in mango juice in the English booth. He was greatly amused and after that, whenever he came to Geneva for a conference, he brought me a hand-woven basket full of carefully-packed mangoes. A very kind man.

My children and I went on a happy mango diet for a few days. They probably thought everyone did the same and this was quite normal. As normal as eating caviar and pistachios every time I came back from an orthopaedic conference in Teheran.

## PART 3  CANBERRA

\* \* \*

I also worked quite often in China during this period. I remember in particular, on one occasion my business class flight had been booked on the first official Chinese airlines (CAC) flight since China had taken over from what had formerly been a Qantas flight, from Sydney to Beijing. The plane was half empty, but there seemed to be an army of dainty, smiling air hostesses to greet us.

Once everyone was seated, a smiling young woman asked me if I would like to move to first class since there were so many vacant seats. Delighted, I climbed the spiral staircase to the top and ensconced myself indulgently in a row of empty seats, ready to be pampered.

Once we were in the air and our champagne, savouries, lobster salad and pavlova had been served, however, the staff all disappeared to the lower level; you could call for an attendant until kingdom come, you would not be heard, and from the sounds below it was obvious that a wild party was taking place.

Then the film began. There were no headphones. The old-fashioned black and white Chinese film that appeared on the one screen in the front of the cabin was in Mandarin; there were no subtitles and the volume was turned up to the maximum. And there was no one to complain to. That night was one of aural torture.

Since that memorable flight, I always check my earplugs are in my travel bag.

Those first conferences in China, mostly in Beijing, took place before tourism took over and before the events of Tiananmen Square. The roads were crowded with hordes of frail-looking bicycles, propelled by young and old and carrying enormous loads. The few cars to be seen were mostly old-fashioned black ones with darkened windows, driving government officials through town, or rather dilapidated taxis with windows that would not close and door handles that rattled and gave the impression they might fall off at any moment.

Sitting outside the Kunlun Hotel having breakfast with a group of colleagues, the street scene was a lesson about life in China. Many of the bicycles pulled wooden carts and I watched a very thin man of about forty pedalling across the square, dragging an old wooden cart carrying four refrigerators. A peasant on a rusty old bicycle had what looked like fifty or so cauliflowers in a net, somehow balanced on the pillion seat, while smart businessmen had document cases, and elegant, modern young women on shiny new bicycles had gloves and handbags. Some of the carts were pulled by men and women on foot.

There was the occasional accident: a bent and broken bicycle lying in the middle of the road, its rider motionless beside it, a stream of blood coming from his head, while a crowd gathered round to look, and taxis and a constant stream of bicycles drove past unconcernedly. Even after several days, watching the traffic and catching taxis, I still couldn't work out which side of the road they were supposed to be on — they seemed to use the middle of the road.

A number of old wooden carts, piled high with some dark-coloured substance, were being pulled along by wrinkled, bent, tired-looking figures who had obviously already been walking for hours; I wondered what it was they were carrying right through the middle of town — until one day one came right next to my taxi window and I was able to see and smell that it was a pile of manure. This aroused my curiosity. Later, when visiting the Great Wall, I had a charming university student as a guide, a Mr Wu, whose English was good enough to answer my questions; he explained that the poorer peasants living in the country sometimes had nothing else to sell.

One of the nicest things that happened during our stay occurred while the interpreters were all having breakfast together one morning, when a thin, elderly lady with white hair went plodding past, dragging a cart of manure across the square. My Spanish booth colleague sitting next to me, Melanie, tall, slim, blonde and beautiful, jumped up, and grabbing her handbag ran out to help. They made a strange couple, the bent Chinese woman in rags and sprightly Melanie in her elegant New York clothes, her curly blonde hair down to her shoulders. Fortunately, she wasn't scheduled to interpret until that afternoon; when she got back to the conference, we all gathered round to hear what she had to tell. Apparently, they had pushed the cart right through town and then out into the countryside and across fields to a primitive hut, where a man had paid the little old lady with some coins. Melanie had thought the 'garbage' on the cart was for compost, but it must have been to feed pigs because the hut was surrounded by them. The old lady allowed Melanie to take photographs of her standing in front of the hut, surrounded by the pigs, to show her small daughter back home.

We were all very touched by what Melanie had done.

Out of habit I often tried to tip taxi drivers, hotel porters or doormen but regretted it because they appeared shocked, startled, even embarrassed and ashamed. Although they refused in no uncertain terms, they still looked over their shoulder to make sure no one had seen.

Mr Wu told me that The Great Wall had taken 200 years to build, 2,500 years ago. The builders' lives were very hard: they were too poor to have warm clothes and they were not given enough food. When they died, they were not even given a proper burial but were just laid under the next piece of wall to be built. Apparently, there was a beautiful maiden who married a man in hiding because he did not want to have to build the wall. Three days after their wedding ceremony, however, soldiers came to take him away to force him to work on it. The maiden made him some warm clothes and then went out looking for him so that she could give them to him. Unfortunately, when at last she found out where he was, he had just died. Soon after, the Emperor happened to be crossing that way. He fell in love with her — she was, apparently, very beautiful — and he wanted to marry her. She agreed, upon condition that her husband be given a proper burial and mourning, and that in the future, all labourers working on the wall would be given the same. The wedding ceremony took place and when it was over, she threw herself from the highest part of the wall. Pilgrims still go there to pray for the souls of those buried under the wall.

On Sundays it seemed everyone went to the park for a magic show. My guide offered to escort me there, together with his girlfriend. We sat on collapsible wooden stools round floor matting which represented the stage and saw demonstrations of kung fu, wood chopping on another recumbent man's chest, even fine onion chopping with a very sharp knife on another man's chest; men rolling about on the ground on broken glass, on upturned chopper blades, bending steel rods round their necks, by placing them beneath their Adam's apple and leaning forward until a deep indent in their neck appeared. I had to look away, for fear I might faint. There were also sword-swallowers and conjurors of all sorts. Looking round, I saw that I was the only non-Chinese person present. As a result, the performers came and bowed to me before beginning their performance and I had to check the knife was sharp and that the onions were truly chopped. My guide took great care of me, keeping me out of the sun, helping me up and down steps and across roads. But when we got back to my hotel, they refused any payment, saying they had learnt so much English from me they felt they should rather pay me! They added that they felt I was more like a family member than a tourist, which I took to be a great compliment!

I invited them for a coffee and some tinned fruit salad in the hotel café, which they seemed to enjoy enormously, as well as being able to 'take advantage of the hotel toilets.' This is something all taxi drivers and guides seemed anxious to do, usually keeping me waiting ten minutes while they did so. Personally, outside the hotel I never had any trouble finding the toilet in restaurants or anywhere else: all you had to do was follow your nose. My only problem was in actually being able to steel myself to use the toilet, once I had found it.

The young people I met were all friendly, bright and intelligent, well-educated and very much aware. I met no lazy or overweight students, no one wearing untidy or neglected clothes. Mr Wu told me he had never been out of China; he had learnt English at evening school over three years. He explained that, like most young people in China, he was very enthusiastic about being able to study because the previous generation had not had that opportunity — they had had to work in the fields to help produce food and construct buildings for the Chinese people. Study was a luxury for them — there weren't enough hours in the day for them to learn all China's history and geography, literature, poetry, music and art. They told me about the Television University available to all, nine hours every day, with thousands of students enrolled.

From my hotel window, early every morning, I saw groups

of people gathering together on every available patch of grass and along the riverbanks to practise tai chi.

Driving round the countryside during the weekends I saw women workers in the fields, two to a shovel — something I had never seen before. They stood in two rows, facing one another: one pushed while the other pulled by means of a heavy rope tied to the handle of the shovel.

After work one evening I took a taxi to the Friendship Store to buy some souvenirs (which were not wrapped in paper but placed in delightful hand-woven pochettes). I asked the taxi to wait, which is what everyone does. The result is a crowd of hooting taxis when you come out of the store and stand on the steps, trying to remember which driver is yours, while they look on anxiously to ensure no other taxi takes their fare. Mr Wu explained that the government did everything possible to discourage people from buying cars because of the enormous number of people on the streets. He kept using the word 'meritorious,' which must be a much-used word in Mandarin. I tried, in vain, to find him a simpler word, easier for him to pronounce (especially in view of the difficulty he had in distinguishing between the 'l' and the 'r' — whenever I asked for the bill in a restaurant, the waiter brought me a beer ...)

At the end of the conference, in the taxi taking me from the hotel to the airport, I realised I still had some Chinese money left in my purse and asked the driver to stop when I saw an antique shop, to see if they had something small I could buy with my remaining *yuan*. I found the perfect thing:

a musical instrument to add to my collection. It looked like a miniature violin with a beautifully carved flower design on the front. I stuffed it into my hand luggage and forgot all about it.

Instead of flying straight to Sydney, my plane stopped first in Melbourne, where we had to identify our luggage out on the tarmac and be sniffed by sniffer dogs before we could fly the last leg home. It seemed customs had received a tip-off that someone on board might be carrying drugs.

When I unpacked the next day, I discovered what I had bought was not a musical instrument at all. The delicate carved flower design was of poppies' seed capsules. The top was in fact just a lid. Opening it, inside I found scales for weighing opium — quite a lot of a mysterious greyish powder had collected in all the corners.

I wonder whether the customs officials would have believed my story if they had found it in my luggage upon arrival at Sydney airport?

It was around this time, during my six months in Geneva, six months in Australia years, that I worked for a series of congresses of the International Council of Nurses. I particularly remember one that took place in Seoul, in the Olympic Stadium, where twelve thousand nurses were present. Buses took us from our hotel to the Stadium every morning and back again at the end of the working day. I remember, one evening on the bus, hearing my own voice, loud and clear, coming from the seat behind me. I couldn't help turning around. A plump nurse from some exotic country was replaying the day's discussions, which she had recorded on her tape recorder, quite illegally because in fact copyright provisions applied. But I didn't have the heart to say anything; she obviously needed to hear it all again. Still, it was a curious sensation to hear one's own voice talking confidently about something one doesn't really know much about.

I remember, too, the passionate plea from a nurse from Peru and that of a nurse from Australia. The Peruvian nurse was asking for Wellington boots. She wanted all nurses to be issued with Wellington boots.

She rose to her feet and, with every minute, her voice rose in pitch; saying her words I felt the same emotion, as we explained that there was blood all over the floor in the operating theatre and the nurses were afraid of getting AIDS.

By the time I had finished, I felt emotionally drained.

Then it was the turn of the nurse from Australia. She was equally passionate; her demand was that nurses not be required to lift weights greater than 20 kg.

Back in Geneva for my Swiss six months, it seemed strange not to be living in my own house. I had booked a room at the Ramada Hotel instead. It was my birthday in July and for the first time for many years I could not have a garden party to celebrate.

Handing in my key one morning as I left for work, I noticed a dozen dark red, long-stemmed Baccara roses in a tall vase on the counter at reception, their scent filling the air. When I commented to the receptionist she explained: 'A contented client, no doubt. They were just addressed to the hotel, not to anyone in particular. They are beautiful, aren't they?'

It wasn't until Peter telephoned a few days later that I understood. 'Did you receive the roses?' he asked. He had forgotten to mention my name or room number …

*   *   *

My next conference was for the Food and Agriculture Organisation in Rome and it was a joy to meet up again with a group of colleagues I hadn't seen for a while. We had a lot of catching up to do.

Walking down the street in Rome I felt a 'real woman' again. The appraising glances from the men passing by, made me feel appreciated. I didn't want wolf-whistles or discourteous suggestions, I certainly didn't want to be touched, I just wanted to be appreciated. The look of approval a man gives a woman was what I missed so much in Australia. The 'blokey' thing to do here was drink beer and crack jokes, thumping one another on the back from time to time and the justification for this, especially if any sport was on the horizon, was that they were 'bonding'. Perhaps the truth of the matter was that Australian men were intimidated by women or uncomfortable in their presence. I have never felt any reaction from men in Anglo-Saxon or Asian countries. In the early days, when walking down a busy street in Australia, I sometimes wondered whether something was wrong — perhaps my skirt was too long or my outfit unflattering. Gradually I came to understand that Anglo-Saxon men were inhibited until they had had a drink or two. Then they went from one extreme to the other, making comments about one's bosom or turning into obnoxious 'touchers'. This was in 1980 — fortunately things have changed since then, thanks to European immigration. In Italy, France or Spain men like to be with women, they know how to talk with them and even flirt a little, in a flattering, gallant way which makes them feel appreciated; that it was worthwhile to have made an extra effort with their hair, put on a little make-up, choosing clothes that suited them … whereas in Australia this seemed a waste of time because no one noticed or cared. Even the local Italo-Australians seemed to have become 'australianised'.

It was very different in Spain where the *piropo* was considered an art form and was, happily, widespread. The only English equivalent I can think of is 'to pay a compliment' but this is a very feeble translation. In the case of the piropo there is no physical contact. It is stylish and elegant. Short and pithy yet poetic and spoken with a sparkle in the eye, a smile, and a look of appreciation — frequently accompanied by a courteous, old-fashioned bow.

To cross a busy road in the heart of Madrid, Granada or Seville you would be waiting for the traffic lights to change and eyeing the people on the other side of the street who were also waiting to cross. When the lights changed, the man coming towards you would say his piropo and then he was gone, never to be seen again. That was it. But if the words had been well chosen, they would stay with you all day. I think the best one I received was from a small man with shining brown eyes full of mischief. As soon as he was close enough for me to hear he said: 'I would like to eat strawberries and cream out of your dimples.' Then he was gone, never to be seen again. And I felt on top of the world.

Another beautiful piropo I received more recently was from a dashing Argentinian delegate at a conference in Australia during the coffee break. As he walked past me in the crowd, he whispered in my ear in Spanish: 'May I please have one of your eyelashes?' I must have looked puzzled. 'To sweeten my coffee ...' he explained, smiling, with a bow.

Dare I daydream that, with more immigrants from Spanish-speaking countries, the art of the piropo may one day find its place in Australia? It is a world away from all this self-righteous talk of sexual harassment. Why are men so different in Anglo-Saxon countries? Why do they try to pinch your bottom or touch your breast? Do they have no poetry in their souls? How I enjoyed having doors opened for me, being made to go first, given flowers and paid poetic compliments with a bow. And a smile — smiles all round. All this sordid 'sexual harassment' is so grim, compared to a little light flirtation. I must confess, I liked it when a man said, 'nice legs!' as I went past, or 'pretty dress!' I enjoy compliments, they make me feel good, they make me feel a real woman. What is wrong with that? I hope the pendulum will swing back, as time goes by, so that being paid a compliment by a man is not considered to be sexual harassment ...

\* \* \*

The last thing I did before leaving Geneva, en route for Canberra via Fiji, was to telephone Astrid to enquire about Arian, who had been on a hunger strike. 'He's in hospital,' she said. 'He didn't want to go. But he was too weak to argue. He's being fed through a tube. He's still weak but he is slightly better.'

Poor Arian! And he thought he had found a way out ...

\* \* \*

Then came another conference for the FAO in Suva. It was good to be back in the Fijian sunshine. *Quinquereme* was still at the Tradewinds and Rocky was waiting at reception to welcome me, having received my message. His golliwog halo of hair was the same but he looked thinner and paler, which seemed to accentuate his sensitive face. Without stopping to unpack, I grabbed the coffee beans I had brought from my suitcase, washed my face and hands, combed my hair and we were off to the Yacht Club. They now had another daughter with the delightful name of Marigold, five years younger than Echo. But Julia had been diagnosed with high blood pressure and had gone to New Zealand for a health check-up, taking the two girls with her.

Rocky seemed to know everyone in the Yacht Club and even had his favourite seat reserved at the bar. To my amazement he ordered a 'Claytons' for himself, explaining that he had had to stop drinking because of a liver problem; I said I would have a Claytons too. We talked a lot. He was still working for the same firm. He gave me the impression he was lonely; he seemed sadly to have lost his sparkle. He hated living on his own and was hoping Julia would come back to Suva in a month or two.

Then it was back to the Tradewinds to study the documents for the meeting the following morning, but it wasn't the same without Echo's early morning laughter and squeals of joy as she climbed the rigging above the pool and crashed down into the water with screams of excitement.

\* \* \*

The Qantas flight back to Australia was packed. It was a 747 and there were 457 passengers in all, 425 in economy class, sixteen in business and the same number in first class. It seemed they were all returning home from a football match somewhere — everyone was already quite jolly as they boarded the plane. No sooner had it taken off and the Goldie Hawn film appeared on the screen than a queue started to form down the aisle to fetch beer. It would have been impossible for a steward to come and ask what one wanted — the aisle was far too crowded. There was one continuous procession down one side towards the galley area and another similar one along the other aisle, in the opposite direction. They blocked the view of the screen completely; anyway, all I could hear was their cheerful banter as they called out noisily to one another. They all seemed broad shouldered and brawny, carefree and out for a good time, in no hurry, stopping to greet friends on the way, sometimes staying for a chat, totally ignoring the film I was hoping to watch. Intent on not spilling a drop of the contents of their glass, they held it very carefully with one hand in front, protecting it as if it were a trophy, while they balanced three reserve cans precariously under the other arm. I supposed the second queue must be for the toilet. As time passed, they all looked happier and happier, their faces redder and redder and their greetings to their friends became louder and louder as they elbowed their way along the aisle. Soon, they were all talking at the tops of their voices, the wives as well — it was like being in a packed Saturday-night pub in the sky.

The kindly lady sitting next to me, who told me she was a judge's wife, asked if I would like 'a beer or at least a shandy'.

'My husband will get it for you,' she said and I realised

however desperate I might be for a shandy I would never have been able to make it unassisted.

'No, thank you,' I replied.

'But they'll be running out of beer!' she said, concerned. 'Let him get you a couple and you can keep them until you want them.'

'No thanks. You're very kind,' I said. 'I'll wait till they come around with coffee or tea.'

In fact, it seemed highly improbable that this would ever happen.

'Well, if you're really sure,' she concluded in a most surprised voice and very generously gave me one of her packets of peanuts as a consolation prize.

\* \* \*

I noticed references in the Canberra Times to a National Accreditation Authority for Translators and Interpreters (NAATI) which had just been set up (in September 1977) by the Commonwealth Government to establish professional standards, provide accreditation at various levels and develop a national system of registration and licensing. Their headquarters were in Canberra and there would be a branch in each state.

As a Council member of the International Professional Association of Conference Interpreters (AIIC), I thought I should investigate, so one day I telephoned to make an appointment and went along to see Richard Adcock, the new

Director. Candidates were being tested for accreditation as community interpreters at levels 1, 2 and 3. Levels 1 and 2 were 'language aids' while level 3 was the first professional level. After many letters, telephone calls and personal visits to their offices I was finally given an opportunity to explain conference interpreting to a NAATI Board Meeting. I spent many hours preparing what I should say: There was so much to explain. Starting from scratch to people who had never attended an international conference, never heard simultaneous interpretation, nor had any idea how international conferences or United Nations worked was not easy — especially as most of the NAATI Board members were monolingual. When I arrived clutching my wad of notes, I was shown into the meeting and told that I had a time slot of twenty minutes maximum. I'm afraid I committed the ultimate crime any conference speaker can commit: I spoke as fast as it is humanly possible. I was desperate not to leave out anything important. Fortunately, no one had to interpret what I said.

AIIC Council appointed me their official negotiator with NAATI, and after more meetings, endless discussions, and question-and-answer sessions, 'Level 4 — conference interpreter/translator' was added to the NAATI accreditation structure. I was then asked to serve on a number of committees as well as the Professional Development Board and the French and Spanish language examiner panels.

It was about this time that I received a letter signed by

some fifteen female community interpreters, asking if I would provide an official statement on behalf of AIIC, to allow women interpreters to wear trousers when interpreting.

One member of the NAATI Board at that time was not monolingual — in fact she taught French at TAFE and the CCAE in Adelaide; she also spoke Italian. I refer to Jill, the wife of the then Minister of Health, Neal Blewett. My exposé had been a revelation to her and she was keen to learn more. She travelled frequently to Canberra for NAATI meetings or to accompany her husband; whenever she did, from that day on, we had lunch together. In between mouthfuls I did my best to impart as much information as possible about the international aspects of interpreting and Jill Blewett became my ally. Everyone else I spoke to on the subject gave the impression that what I was talking about was fine for Europe but *'this is Australia, we don't need all that here. We're fine as we are.'*

Jill Blewett, however, was very enthusiastic and keen to bring Australia into the international conference world. She even went so far as to take six months leave to go to Europe, and with my introductions, attended a conference interpretation course at the European Economic Community in Brussels as an observer. Upon her return she was one of the few prominent people in Australia who understood the problems and advantages of implanting the profession and the conference industry here. She was always willing to help me in any way she could. Over lunch I convinced her of the need for a post-graduate training course for European languages in this country. Until we had at least one team of qualified conference interpreters were available, it would be pointless to try to launch the conference industry in Australia. Bringing interpreters and translators from overseas would be far too costly. We therefore set about planning a post-graduate course which, while attached to the Australian National University, would be located in the projected Canberra Convention Centre complex. However, Jill's sudden death in October 1988, was a great loss to the profession and also spelt the end of our plans for an Australian training course in two or three European languages at NAATI Level 4.

* * *

At a private cocktail party one evening in Canberra, I was introduced to a lady who claimed to translate and interpret seventeen languages and to be a qualified conference interpreter. I must have opened my eyes wide in disbelief. What amazed me most was that she had been able to get away with such a story! She told me she had a certificate to prove her qualifications: She had learnt simultaneous interpretation by means of a correspondence course. She didn't seem to realise the impossibility of such a claim. To a professional conference interpreter it sounded like a joke!

She got her come-uppance though. After many years of simultaneous interpretation, my daughter and I can speak as fast as any human being. We cornered her between us and when she said she spoke fluent French, we submerged her in the language in a fast-flowing onslaught until she had a dazed, pathetic, and uncomprehending look. Then we felt she had suffered enough.

A few international conferences had taken place in Australia in the past but all the interpreters had had to be flown out from Europe at great expense, making the conference extraordinarily costly. Then the international organisations definitely decided they could not afford to hold conferences in this country.

Australian diplomats who had attended international conferences with simultaneous interpretation in other countries had no idea how it worked. I well remember being asked to visit a middle-aged gentleman in a government department in Melbourne, who had to organise a telecommunications conference with simultaneous interpretation the following year. He had absolutely no idea how to proceed.

'If only one delegate speaks at a time, then all we need is one interpreter?' he asked.

I spent an hour explaining it all to him in great detail, with diagrams galore: how we are two interpreters per booth and each works half an hour on, half an hour off. At last, when I thought he had understood how it all worked, he said:

'OK I'll take ten.'

'Ten what?' I asked.

'Ten interpreters.'

'Fine,' I said. 'Which languages?'

'I can't tell you that beforehand, can I? How do I know what language they will speak until they take the floor?'

At that point I felt like giving up.

To get the profession started in Australia, the first thing I needed was a good local team for English, French and Spanish in order to demonstrate that it was possible to hold successful conferences here at reasonable cost. I therefore set about travelling all over the country as well as to New Caledonia and New Zealand to ascertain what local skills were available, also lecturing at the language departments of the various universities on the way. I could hardly recommend that would-be interpreters go to train in Europe or America when their families were in Australia, and the cost would be beyond their means, although three, to the best of my knowledge, did manage to do so.

My first meeting with Australian interpreters took place in a private home in Sydney in 1983. The seven would-be professional interpreters present worked as community or court interpreters as well as tour guides and translators; the picture they gave of the conference scene in Australia showed that an enormous gulf existed between status, professional standards and fees compared to those in Europe and America. It was obvious that my first task was to raise standards and improve professionalism, and most of all, quality of performance. I decided my best approach would be to begin by recruiting mixed teams of local and overseas professional interpreters. This would enable the former to learn from the latter and enable a better understanding of the problems facing interpreters in this country. Most beginners say they learn more from working with experienced professionals than from any amount of teaching. By recruiting one or two inexperienced Australian interpreters to work in the booths with colleagues from Europe, and working with local interpreters myself we were able to add the polish that was missing from their performance.

There were no locally organised international conferences planned at that time unfortunately, where I would have been able to listen to the Australian interpreters' performance; the only way to see how they performed was for me to recruit potential interpreters myself in order to assess the quality of their performance — a risky adventure. Fortunately, the international organisations I had been working for in Geneva contacted me whenever they had a conference in the Asia-Pacific region, to ask if I could recommend any local interpreters, as this would considerably cut the cost of the conference.

I am enormously indebted to three colleagues from Europe who actually changed their professional domicile to Australia for the six months concerned so that I could recruit them as locals. This was a wonderful gesture of solidarity and support towards their Australian colleagues and of enormous help to me.

Putting an inexperienced Australian interpreter on a team was not without danger but between us, with the help of those I had recruited from Europe, we somehow managed to cover up when there was a problem. However, I do remember hearing with horror *'el reporte'* from the Spanish booth instead of *'el informe,'* and in an aeronautical conference during a session about air crashes, each time an English-speaking delegate referred to *'injuries'* I heard *'injures'* coming from the French booth which quite took my breath away! Fortunately, the conference organisers and delegates were very forgiving, and out of gratitude for the enormous savings in the conference budget, under the heading 'interpreters' air fares and subsistence allowances' resulted from the use of these local interpreters. Some of the new colleagues were receptive to criticism and suggestions and later prospered, while others were not and were never seen again. Thanks to the patience and support of colleagues from Geneva, Amsterdam and Paris I finally had a local team more or less ready to tackle the Australian conference market. We were on the crest of a wave.

Of the seven original would-be Australian conference interpreters, thanks to the help and patience of my European colleagues, I was able to sponsor one eventually to become a member of our professional association, working in the Spanish booth. Then encouraged another to study conference interpreting at Georgetown University, so that when he came back to Sydney fully qualified, he too was able to become a member of our professional association.

The new NAATI Professional Development Board decided a professional association was needed here to establish professional standards and a Code of Ethics; AUSIT (the Australian Institute of Interpreters and Translators) was set up in September 1987, governed by a National Council comprising a five-member national executive, and one delegate from each of the six state branches. I was asked to be its first President but declined because I had many overseas assignments and would not be spending sufficient time in Australia over the foreseeable future.

I still, however, had an enormous problem in Australia when Japanese was required, which was becoming increasingly frequent. In the late 1970s and early 1980s Japanese delegations brought their own interpreters with them from Japan and their English pronunciation was extremely difficult to understand. Working into French on a number of occasions, taking relay from the Japanese booth's English, I found that, although there was a steady flow of words, there was often no thread to follow. This prompted me to campaign for a Japanese course in simultaneous interpretation for native English-speaking students of Japanese or Australians of Japanese origin.

At that time Australian ministers and industrialists visiting Japan to promote trade relied entirely on the Japanese interpreter provided by their host. This meant that only the part of the discussion they 'needed to know' was interpreted for them. They missed the asides, comments and unofficial exchanges. When I tried to explain that these interpreters' loyalties and interests were with the other side, I was told that this was how it had always been done in the past and that professional, qualified interpreters were too expensive for the Australian delegation to take with them.

But fate was on my side. My prayers were answered by Professor Joyce Ackroyd of the University of Queensland and Peter Davidson, Director of their Japanese Language Proficiency Unit.

Serendipitously, at about that time in 1980, they were thinking about setting up a post-graduate conference interpreting training program, and had contacted the International Association of Conference Interpreters in Geneva to ask for guidance. I received a letter from them entrusting me with the task.

There followed a series of lecture and interpretation workshop trips to St. Lucia, in Brisbane, where I was treated like the Queen of Interpretation and overwhelmed with heart-warming hospitality. There were Japanese dinners at the homes of members of the staff, wonderful picnics, sightseeing trips and excursions, which will stay in my memory for ever. The students were a delight and many of them became friends. It was a real joy to travel from one part of Brisbane to another by ferryboat along the river, far from the 'madding crowd' and busy traffic of the city. There was a ferry stop at the foot of the university campus; my morning trip to work was a delight and what better way to unwind after a busy day than to travel back to my hotel by boat, accompanied by the soothing sound of the rippling water?

In November, the final examinations were to take place for the first time and I was appointed Head of the Jury. Mr

Davidson and Mr Uchiyama met me at Brisbane airport at twelve-thirty and took me to an Italian restaurant for lunch, saying the examinations *'wouldn't start until 2 o'clock.'* They explained that they served two purposes: The Australian MA to be judged by Mr Davidson and Mr Uchiyama, and an international level for which I would be responsible, basing my judgement on NAATI Level 4 accreditation and AIIC pre-candidacy.

'Fine,' I said, as I sat down to lunch and unfolded my table napkin. 'All I need then is your marking procedure. Could I have a copy now, to look at over lunch so as to familiarise myself with it?'

'Oh, we're leaving all that to you,' was the reply. It was as though the heavens had collapsed on to my head.

I remember desperately grabbing a notepad and pen out of my handbag and trying to work out a marking system on the corner of the restaurant table next to my plate of spaghetti. I chose five criteria and a weighting system. When I had finished examining all the students I would go back and compare them with one another, to be sure I was being absolutely fair and not affected by tiredness as the day wore on. I did the best I could at such short notice.

As soon as I got back home in Canberra, I contacted colleague examiners at the Interpretation Schools of Paris (ESIT) and Geneva (ETI) to obtain their marking procedures, which I then melded with my own for future use at Queensland University.

After that, I kept a selection of speeches from conferences

at which I had worked, for use at examinations and for teaching purposes. Colleagues at both Paris and Geneva Universities were also very helpful in offering suggestions for the syllabus.

Fate was kind to me again when I needed to contact a colleague in Japan to join us on the examination panel and come over from time to time to give lectures. Serendipity guided my hand when I chose Kondo. He was an enormous asset to our team, immensely popular with the students and great fun to be with as well. We all enjoyed his company.

Peter Davidson was a wonderful host. Each time I went to St. Lucia I was ensconced in a comfortable hotel and invited out in the evenings to restaurants, to Mr and Mrs Davidson's home, as well as to that of Mr and Mrs Uchiyama — we called him Hiro because his first name was Hiromichi. They took me on magnificent sightseeing trips during the weekends. In November Brisbane was the colour of jacaranda flowers. The trees were ablaze with colour and so were the pavements and grass beneath. Most beautiful of all were the flowers floating on the campus lake. I have wonderful memories of Japanese picnics by the lakeside where delicious Japanese food was served on square black lacquered beflowered plates, leaving me with an impression of extreme elegance and sophistication. That may have been the day an official photograph was taken of us all, standing in a group underneath a jacaranda tree. It wasn't until I saw the printed photograph later that I realised that Kondo, instead of standing behind me, had jumped up into the tree at the last minute and perched himself among the branches. Happy times! Now when I see jacaranda trees in blossom in November my thoughts take me back to St. Lucia and the magic colourful world of jacaranda trees, flowers all over the grass and a floating carpet of them on the lake ...

Mr and Mrs Davidson always gave a lavish barbecue party when the exams were over, inviting the staff and all the students involved. It generally began with Kondo taking a swim in the pool and ended with music. Kondo was on the piano with various instrumentalists joining in including Mr Davidson himself who was also an excellent musician. What happy occasions they were!

One year, however, the examinations became rather sinister. I had instituted a system whereby the students, instead of having to wait several days for the results, could come back later that afternoon or early evening to find out whether they had passed or not. It meant a long day for the examiners — sometimes we didn't finish until 7 or 8 pm — but at least it avoided the agonising waiting period for the students and meant that the examiners finished their task the same day.

On the occasion I have in mind, one of the students was a tall, strong, muscular young man with a shaven head except for a vertical crest of bristle-like hair down the centre of his cranium. He wore a sleeveless singlet, showing off his biceps to advantage and an amazing array of tattoos covering his arms, back and neck. He also had rings piercing his face and body in various places and long dangling earrings.

Unfortunately, he did not do well. He was the last student of the day, which meant that it was quite late when he finally came back for his results. As Head of the Jury it was my task to tell him the verdict.

When I announced that he had unfortunately failed, he exploded.

'But I studied all day yesterday and most of the night!' he expostulated. 'It's not possible that I failed.'

I resisted the temptation to tell him he should have studied throughout the year and not just the last day and night. Instead, I went through each section of the exam, explaining where his marks had been insufficient, repeating what he had said and what he should have said with as much patience as I could muster.

Angry and red-faced, he rose to his feet.

'I know why you've 'failed' me,' he shouted. 'It's because I'm homosexual. And because I'm Aboriginal,' he protested, shouting and raising his fist.

I had had no idea that he was either.

At a loss as to what to do, I sat there helpless, hoping for inspiration. I felt that I had done all I could... I had gone through the entire exam and explained all his insufficiencies and errors. The other jury members were also at a loss; they were waiting in silence to see what I would do. A feeling of uncertainty, even fear, began to take hold.

'I won't let anyone out of this room until I get satisfaction,' he shouted. 'I worked all day and half the night and I deserve to pass!'

We looked at one another in silent consultation. I began to wonder how this would end. The university was quiet — it seemed everyone but us had gone home.

We had reached a deadlock but I was determined not to give in to his threats. In spite of myself, however, a feeling of panic began to engulf me: How could I bring the situation to a satisfactory solution? I imagined the newspaper headlines the following morning: 'Drama at Queensland University ...'

Suddenly, out of the blue, the spell was broken by a group of three young women students bursting into the room. Because of the silence they had thought it was all over and there was no one there. They had been waiting outside to find out how the last candidate had fared. Their solidarity saved the day! In silence we hastily rose to our feet and left, immensely relieved that the tension had been broken.

\* \* \*

I finally succeeded in convincing NAATI that students passing the NAATI accredited MA Japanese interpreting course at the University of Queensland were in fact beginner conference interpreters and should not be placed in the same category as experienced AIIC interpreters who had been practising for more than 200 days (a sine qua non condition of AIIC membership); thus a new Level 5 was created, called 'Senior conference interpreters.' All AIIC members since then, coming to work in Australia or New Zealand, have automatically been accredited at Level 5, the highest level. I had the honour of becoming the first Australian Level 5 interpreter.

By 1985 we had the required fifteen AIIC members in India, Japan, Hong Kong, New Caledonia and Australia to request the creation of a new Asia-Pacific region and I was elected the first Asia-Pacific Council Member.

The simultaneous interpretation equipment supplied for my first conference in Melbourne took my breath away. I hadn't seen anything like it since the old days when I first started interpreting. I had almost forgotten such headphones had ever existed! Not only had they been obsolete in Europe for a number of years but, as the microphone was attached to the earpiece, like those used by telephone operators, each time you grabbed a quick sip of water in the middle of a sentence, you dipped your microphone into the glass.

I had been entrusted with the organisation of the teams of interpreters for a large international telecommunications conference to take place a few months later; this gave me an excellent opportunity to persuade the equipment suppliers to update Australian interpretation equipment. A few judicious telephone calls to their head office in the Netherlands, to the Secretary General of the international organisation concerned in Geneva, and to various high-ranking proudly Australian officials, explaining that more than a thousand delegates from 114 countries would be attending the conference, and how shocked they would be to find such out-of-date equipment used in an affluent country like Australia. This had the desired results. We have had the best and most modern equipment on the market since then.

Afterwards the only remaining problem was that, being monolingual, the technicians insisted upon turning up the volume of the PA system in meeting rooms so that they and everyone else could hear the English channel without headphones making hearing extremely difficult for delegates and interpreters listening to languages other than English. When you enter a conference room with simultaneous interpretation in Europe, you hear nothing until you put on your headphones, which puts all languages on the same footing.

I visited Sydney's wonderful Opera House and found it most impressive with its amazing white sails for a roof and its artistic interior. It seemed people were constantly complaining about its cost but to my mind such a beautiful, unique, artistic building was priceless. I was told it contained an acoustically perfect concert hall with silent seats, made of wood rather than metal to ensure they were noiseless, as well as a modern auditorium with highly perfected acoustics, which could also be used as a conference venue because it was provided with 'a radio system' and interpretation booths. When I went to investigate, however, they were a great disappointment: The booths were extremely small with room for only one person, which meant they were useless. As a result, each time I organised an international conference in the prestigious Opera House, I had to hire temporary booths to be placed at the back of the auditorium while the built-in booths remained empty.

After a lecture tour on the subject of the new conference industry and how it would boost Australia's economy, as well as the need for modern international-standard conference centres in this country, a series of letters to various newspapers and a full-page interview in *The Australian*, I was asked to vet the plans for the first Australian convention centre to be built in Adelaide. I was also to act as consultant regarding others to be built in Melbourne, Sydney (Darling Harbour), Brisbane and Cairns, which was very exciting. Then the news broke that a convention centre was also to be built in the nation's capital: a trump card for Canberra, and an important milestone in the career of the architect, who designed a beautiful white building with very few windows and all the latest gadgets but no simultaneous interpretation booths.

'We can always add those later if we find we need them' I was told when I enquired.

Besides, the new building would be more than a mere conference centre: To be profitable it had to be 'multi-purpose' (the new 'in' word) so that it could be used for weddings, motor and gardening shows and other such events. I tried to explain that if they made it too 'multi-purpose' it might end up being unsuitable for any of them and undertook another lecture tour on the subject 'Do not build a white elephant'. Finally, I was able to convince the architect to add interpretation booths.

I wrote to the architect to ask if we could meet but he declined. His secretary explained over the telephone that he did not want any interference: He knew best what was required.

Something had to be done. An enormous hole had been excavated on the building site and adjacent to it was the glass-fronted architect's office. Parking my car outside I could see the Convention Centre plans on the secretary's desk among a pile of other papers. I knew she must leave the office sometime to make coffee, go to the toilet or to lunch I waited patiently until she did. As quickly and quietly as possible I slipped through the glass door, 'borrowed' the plans and made off with them. My law-abiding husband, who was sitting beside me, was very upset at what I had done, and even more so when I asked him to hurry off and make photocopies while I kept watch. Because they were not A4 size they could not be photocopied in any of the usual places and it was some time before he came back with the copies and I could sneak in and replace the original plans during another of the secretary's trips to the toilet. My poor law-abiding Australian husband was almost apoplectic!

In fact, I was not afraid of being caught; that could only be to my advantage from the point of view of publicity. I would have been delighted to be taken to court; this would have given me an opportunity to state my case and have it reported in all the newspapers. Unfortunately, however, I got off scot-free.

AIIC Technical Committee in Geneva did an excellent job with the photocopies I sent them of the plans, and sent back five pages of possible improvements regarding the siting of the interpretation booths, the need for extra toilets for the interpreters, and most important of all, the need for the interpretation booths to have large windows enabling a full panoramic view of the meeting room. I sent these to the architect's office with a humble, very polite, letter, and as a result, interpretation booths were added and a few of our minor suggestions were taken into account.

However, when the new Canberra Convention Centre opened in 1989, and the interpreters arrived for the first international conference to be held there (The Non-Proliferation of Chemical Weapons), we found the booths to be unusable. Instead of the usual large glass windows enabling us to see all speakers clearly, all we had were small horizontal windows way above our heads. To be able to see the delegates we would have had to stand for the whole working day, and even then, we would not have a clear view of all the speakers.

So, the opening of the conference had to be delayed while temporary booths were installed in the back of the conference room; before the next international conference with simultaneous interpretation could be held there, and the floor had to be raised so that the interpreters could see out of the windows.

It was not an easy job to implant the conference interpreting profession in Australia and combat prevailing ignorance. I even heard: *'Why pay so much for a professional interpreter when the tea-lady speaks Italian?'*

Brisbane's *Courier Mail* published such a story on 2 March 1989:

'An Immigration, Local Government and Ethnic Affairs Department spokesman, Mr Doug Callaghan, said yesterday the commission had asked for an Italian interpreter at 1 pm on Wednesday. 'We couldn't find anybody at such short notice, which led the court to recruit the cleaner,' Mr Callaghan said.

A court official gave her $29.75 for her appearance yesterday, but Mrs Cannizzaro refused to take it until told she had to. *'I was scared and frightened I would make a mistake that would get me in big trouble,'* she said.

As an interpreter, it is not often that words fail me. An Italian cleaner working as an interpreter in an Australian court! I hope the accusation wasn't too serious a matter.

Margaret O'Toole, Judge of the Compensation Court of New South Wales, explained to me that justice must not only be done; it must also be seen to be done. It is for this reason that some court officers believe that 'any interpreter is better than none.' In other words, justice may appear to be done if an interpreter is present, however unqualified and unsatisfactory he/she may be — and however 'affordable'. Using a less expensive unqualified or incompetent interpreter is of course grossly unfair to non-English speaking people whose personal liberty may be at stake, as well as to their English-speaking opponents or co-defendants. In such cases it would be better to have no interpreter at all because of the dangerous consequences of mistakes and misunderstandings and the fact that various protagonists might trust the words of the interpreter without realising that he/she is incompetent.

I kept telling people that having an incompetent interpreter is worse than having no interpreter at all, just as having a clock telling you the wrong time is worse than having no clock at all, but no one believed me. They insisted that having someone, however incompetent, was better than having no one. And an unqualified interpreter was so much cheaper than a professional one. How wrong they were!

It was fortunate for me, that when I lived in Canberra, Bob Hawke became Prime Minister: He was familiar with simultaneous and consecutive interpretation and knew how to use them to his advantage because for many years he had relied upon interpretation at the International Labour Conference held every June in Geneva (where mine was often the voice he heard in his earphones). From experience, he knew how to make himself clearly understood and express himself in a way that facilitated translation into other languages, whereas those who followed him as Prime Minister unfortunately completely failed to understand this. They seemed to think that the more Australian slang they used, the more Australian they sounded, the better it was. However, they were the losers if the audience couldn't understand what they were talking about; it was in everyone's interests to speak 'middle of the road' English and be understood by all.

Some years later, instead of taking his own Australian interpreter with him, for example, John Howard frequently used the interpretation services provided by his host country when travelling overseas, which meant that he was not getting the full picture — he was being told what the other party wanted him to hear. Had he taken an Australian Chinese-speaking interpreter with him, for example, to China, everything would have been translated for him, even unofficial comments. Obviously, interpreters take their instructions from those who recruit and pay them.

Bob Hawke also appreciated the fact that consecutive interpretation gave him a few minutes in which to think and prepare what he was going to say next. Some speakers proudly declined interpretation, like General de Gaulle many years before, thinking they knew enough of the other language to get by. Even if they do, however, consecutive interpretation gives them the advantage of that useful pause.

To complete the De Gaulle story: As a result of declining the services of an interpreter, he proceeded to upset the English by 'demanding' this and that, instead of 'asking' as one would say in English — thinking, mistakenly, that 'demander' in French was 'demand' in English.

I enjoyed working in Parliament House for Mr Hawke; he was not only articulate and easy to follow, he was often unpredictable which kept me on my toes, as did his fertile sense of humour. He was unconventional and innovative. He made witty comments, frequently providing me with an opportunity for mental acrobatics. A good sense of humour goes a long way to oil the machinery particularly in delicate discussions on a sensitive subject. His sentences were often long and entangled, but he always came out happily at the end, to the great relief of his interpreter. I liked too, the fact that he was a consensus leader, like the Pacific Islanders, rather than the usual majority vote Anglo-Saxon politicians.

At least we didn't have the problems George Bush's interpreters must have had with his malapropisms, such as 'I am very gracious and humbled' when expressing his thanks to supporters. 'A tax cut is really one of the anecdotes to coming out of an economic illness.' 'I am a person who recognises the fallacy of humans.' 'We cannot let terrorist or rogue nations hold this nation hostile or hold our allies hostile.' Interpreters are supposed to translate exactly what the speaker says ...

Or Al Gore's interpreters who had to contend with 'It's time for the human race to enter the solar system' and 'I stand by all the misstatements I've made.'

Whereas most Australian politicians in those days — and most Australian men in general — wore shapeless suits with baggy trousers, Bob Hawke dressed more like European men; I particularly liked his white suits. Australian men rarely wore white suits. When I knew him, he was already silvery-grey haired and one of the few people I know who was more handsome at fifty than when he was younger, according to the photographs I have seen.

I was also very impressed with the fact that he remained strictly teetotal throughout his prime ministership — a triumph of willpower.

I heard him referred to as a 'great burst of sunshine on the political scene;' I felt that he radiated authenticity. I think one of the truest descriptions of him I have encountered is that of Barrie Cassidy many years later, who said he was an 'intellectual knockabout.'

I liked working for Barry Jones, too. He was kind, considerate and fatherly as well as erudite and clear-thinking; his jerky delivery was compensated for by the fact that he knew how to place his voice, which carried across the room with clarity. Also, he was always appreciative of our efforts and seemed to be the only politician who understood what our work entailed; most seemed to think we were some sort of language robot who could effortlessly churn out whatever language was required, at the drop of a hat.

I admired Gareth Evans too; he was not only an excellent diplomat but also extremely erudite — whatever the subject under discussion he always had the facts and figures at his fingertips and offered them in a quiet, polite, calming voice.

I remember a high-level ministerial meeting in Parliament House, Canberra: a pale nervous lady sat next to the Prime Minister, fidgeting endlessly with the papers in front of her and dropping her pencil on the floor several times. I had been recruited by the Quai d'Orsay to work for the visiting French Prime Minister. During the coffee break she came across to express her admiration for what I was doing and ask if I minded continuing interpreting both ways non-stop. When I asked her what her role there was, she confessed she was the Australian Prime Minister's interpreter but she had only been told at 4 o'clock the previous afternoon so had had little time to prepare and had not slept a wink that night. 'In any case,' she added, 'I couldn't do what you do. I was sent here because I've just got back from a posting in Paris. I can ask my way in the street or order in a restaurant, but I could never hope to understand the finer shades of meaning of an intricate technical or diplomatic discussion or delicate trade negotiations when the speakers are eloquent and highly knowledgeable in their specialised subject.'

In other words, both sides were dependent on the interpretation provided and paid for by the visiting foreign statesman! Shame!

Fortunately, things have changed since then; gradually the powers have realised that there are different levels of understanding of a foreign language and that interpretation is a skill of its own.

The first time I worked for Bob Hawke in Parliament House, in the early 1980s, a welcome cocktail party had been organised the first evening. 'See you tonight at the party!' someone said to me as I prepared to leave. 'I haven't been invited,' I said, picking up my handbag to go. One of the staff members standing nearby stepped forward and explained: 'I'm afraid we couldn't invite you because there's no ladies' toilet in the prime ministerial part of the building.' Before anyone could say another word, Mr Hawke declared in a loud voice: 'I hereby invite our interpreter to the party and she may use the Prime Minister's toilet.' That settled the matter.

From that day on, Bob Hawke could do no wrong in

my eyes. It wasn't that I so desperately wanted to go to the party, rather that I felt I had been discriminated against as a woman. Thanks to him, I had achieved a small victory on behalf of all women.

I hadn't forgotten, too, that he had been awarded the United Nations Media Peace Prize in 1980, what a good dancer he was and how well we had danced together in Geneva … Maybe I was still under the influence of his aftershave …

In difficult situations, he was quite defiant; I never once saw him weaken.

Old Parliament House was small, compact and had a cosy, informal atmosphere although it was full of history. Moving to new Parliament House in 1988 came as a shock; its cold, impersonal, endless shiny pale green-grey corridors were daunting, particularly if you were wearing high heels. It took me a while to work out which lift went to which floor and which areas were therefore inaccessible by means of which lifts.

In August 1989 the Prime Minister of France, M. Michel Rocard visited Australia with Mme Rocard and the Minister for Foreign Affairs, Mme Avice, both very sophisticated, elegant, beautifully coiffed and perfumed ladies. They all arrived one Friday morning at 7.30 am at Canberra airport together with thirty-five representatives of the French media. As their interpreter I had to be part of the reception committee waiting to greet them.

We visited new Parliament House in the company of

Prime Minister Bob Hawke, with guards of honour in red uniforms on one side and blue on the other. Both national anthems were sung followed by a selection of French songs by a choir of schoolchildren from Canberra's French school. All this proceeded like clockwork, helping us recover from the demonstration that had taken place as we drove up towards the entrance, where there had been crowds on either side of the road all the way, as well as gathered outside Parliament House, a great deal of shouting, megaphones, banners and large placards with 'Frenchies Go Home'. Tomatoes were thrown at us and at our cars and some yellow material meant to be 'yellow cake,' which the *Canberra Times* said later was 'rock hard'. I believe the police made four arrests: Apparently the throwing was not authorised — the demonstration had been authorised provided nothing was thrown. Australian feelings still ran high about the French nuclear tests on Mururoa.

Everywhere I went with the official party we had to protect ourselves from tomatoes and other objects thrown at us, and our twenty sleek white Commonwealth cars were soon covered with it all, which must have given M. and Mme Rocard an unusual welcome. I must confess, too, that I found the Australian journalists extremely rude, aggressive and provocative, compared to their counterparts in Europe.

Discussions were held with cabinet ministers and afterwards everyone rushed to the cars to drive in pomp to the National Press Club for lunch; the afternoon consisted of speeches, questions and answers at Parliament House and the day ended with a reception at the French Embassy. The second day was much the same and included a visit to CSIRO.

Travelling in the second car in the motorcade, the one behind that of the French Prime Minister himself, flying the *tricolor*, was quite exciting — we had a white-helmeted police escort on white motorbikes in front and on either side of our car, blue lights flashing, sirens sounding, as we drove from the airport to Parliament House and from one meeting place to another. There were several AFP bodyguards — mine was a tall, muscular, thick-set young man with whom I had quite interesting conversations during the long intervals spent waiting.

I did wonder whether a tiny flicker in Bob Hawke's memory occurred when he saw me — did he say to himself 'I know that face from somewhere — 'Perhaps I danced with her in a restaurant in Geneva?' Probably not ...

After the reception at *La Résidence* I was glad to be home by eight-thirty and not to have to attend the dinner at The Lodge, because the following morning I had to be up at 4 o'clock. It was the day of the national airline pilots' strike and I had been instructed to be at the Hyatt hotel, where all the visitors were staying, to catch a special bus that would be leaving for Sydney at 5 am.

Most of us slept during the bus trip to Sydney; towards the latter part, as people started waking up and talking to one another, I found I was surrounded by journalists from Reuters, staff from Foreign Affairs in Canberra and members of the French media. As we approached the Regent Hotel in Sydney there was a kerfuffle in the back of the bus as the men changed into their suits, collars and ties. Upon arrival we were ushered into the breakfast room for a 'Sunriser,' which turned out to be fresh orange and lime juice with honey, egg and nutmeg and was absolutely delicious and most refreshing.

Then we went upstairs to a meeting between Treasurer Keating and Michel Rocard and a group of business representatives, all anxious to secure their share of the European single market as of 1992. After more questions and answers at another press conference, we were off to Campbell Cove steps to board the MV John Cadman III for lunch. There were four police boats surrounding us as we tucked into our Tasmanian sea trout with medallions of lobster and roast lamb with hot beetroot sauce, followed by cheese and fruit.

Then an afternoon of discussions at the Regent Hotel, after which we were taken by bus to the airport to wave goodbye to the French visitors, who caught a plane to New Caledonia, while I boarded the bus for a four-hour drive back to Canberra, only to be invited, instead, thankfully, at the last minute, to board Paul Keating's private RAAF plane which was much more comfortable!

I sat opposite Mr Keating for most of the trip and we chatted, but once again unfortunately, I have no recollection whatsoever of what we talked about.

Upon arrival at Fairbairn RAAF base in Canberra, we

were met by white Commonwealth cars to take us to the Hyatt. From there I telephoned home to ask my husband if he could pick me up at the Hyatt Hotel. The trip should have taken him about ten minutes but in fact he arrived one and a half hours later: I suspect a high-speed last-minute house clean and tidy-up. When he finally arrived, he found me asleep on a sofa in the foyer ...

※　※　※

It was in February 1990, that a meeting of the 'Club Australie' was scheduled to take place at Parliament House — which was surrounded by trucks and 'truckies' protesting about something or other and blocking all entrances. Everyone had to park outside the barricades and walk the last ten minutes, which we found most annoying. Especially for those of us wearing high heels. The truckies were waiting for the arrival of the Prime Minister, Bob Hawke.

We managed to cheat them, however, by going down to the car park unobtrusively, after removing our badges (passes to Parliament House); private cars were waiting for the 'skeleton staff' to take us to the French Embassy where the meeting had been secretly rescheduled. The Prime Minister had been driven direct to the French Embassy; we were all very proud of ourselves to think, that while we were holding our meeting, the truckies were still waiting for us outside Parliament House!

It was a gentle sunny day; in the room at the Embassy

where our meeting was held, the French windows were wide open, looking out onto a manicured lawn and rosebushes laden with beautiful roses. The pretty flowery curtains fluttered occasionally; from time to time we could hear lazy summer bird calls. In the background were delicate, white-barked trees, the branches of which seemed to have been arranged by some mysterious hand as if the trunk were a vase. A perfect setting for harmonious discussions.

\* \* \*

During the period he was Treasurer, Paul Keating described his opponents as harlots, sleazebags, frauds, immoral cheats, blackguards, pigs, mugs, clowns, criminal intellects, box heads, corporate crooks, friends of tax cheats, brain-damaged, loopy crims, stupid foul-mouthed grubs, pieces of criminal garbage, clots, fops, gigolos, shags on a rock, 24-carat fogies, dullards, mindless, hare-brained hillbillies, ninnies, thugs, dimwits, muck, rip-off merchants, constitutional vandals, barnyard bullies, and gutless spivs. One of my favourites was 'laughing gas sniffers;' I hoped this description would come up when I was interpreting for him as I had found a good translation for it, but unfortunately my waiting was in vain.

By the time he became Prime Minister in 1991, I had had some practice with his quick wit and sharp tongue. Working for him was never dull — every day presented new challenges. One was his habit of leaving sentences dangling in mid-air. Unfinished sentences are a problem for interpreters — we are so afraid our listeners will think it is our fault, and that we have lost the end of the sentence. We don't get a chance to explain that there wasn't one. And much as we would like to and probably could, it is not within our mandate to finish the sentence for the speaker.

My main problem though, was his amazing, unconventional and emotional vocabulary which the English-speaking part of my brain relished, while the non-English part was being put to the test. How does one interpret into formal, prime ministerial French or Spanish such expressions as: 'it's all pig-swill,' 'rubbery figures,' 'it's a two-bob each way situation,' 'ballpark figures,' 'double dipping,' 'getting on the gravy train,' 'having a blue,' 'scumbag,' 'ratbag,' 'galah,' 'too many snouts in the trough,' 'toe-rag' and 'they're having a barney in the Middle-East.' Translated into French or Spanish they all sounded very strange and not always polite. 'Razor-gang' sounded extremely bloodthirsty in Russian. 'I can hear an ant change step' fascinated me, being a dancer. I could just picture that pretty little ant dancing the cha-cha-cha. It was fun searching for an equivalent in other languages for 'ratbaggery'. But I did wonder whether the French Prime Minister pondered during his long flight home, over the mysteries of Sydney Harbour and what could possibly be hidden there. It was easy enough to translate 'bottom of the harbour scheme' into other languages, but the words would have been quite meaningless to the listener, who must have concluded that Australians use their harbours for strange, nefarious purposes. The simultaneous or consecutive interpreter of course has no time to stop and explain: 'an illegitimate or illegal means of disposing of company assets.' Alas! It is all we can do to keep up with the speaker and come to the end of the sentence at the same time, in order not to miss whatever comes next.

I delighted in searching for an equivalent in French and Spanish for 'He's a cherry on top of a compost heap.' 'Investment shot through the roof' sounds very strange in French, as does 'the interest rate literally took the stuffing out of the place.' 'A wink and a nod deal,' and 'Downer is a sook.' How on earth could one say 'sook' in Russian, Spanish or even French, without sounding extremely impolite?

It is a problem when speakers use fair dinkum Australianisms rather than middle-of-the-road English because delegations such as those from India, Pakistan, Sri Lanka, Thailand, Myanmar, Kenya, Norway, Sweden, Denmark, Finland as well as the United States of America and Canada are all listening to the English channel and may not have any idea what the Australian delegate is talking about. Non-English-speaking delegates are more fortunate because they hear the interpreter, who may have come across those expressions before and have some idea of their meaning. Surely, when speaking to delegates of other countries, one's aim should be to be understood, rather than to show off how Australian one is.

The President of Argentina must have wondered why people living in Republics eat so many bananas.

Another thing I noticed about Australian politicians was their continual attack on their own opposition when speaking with foreign statesmen, as if the latter were familiar with Australia's domestic affairs. Even when making speeches abroad, they still attack the opposing party at every opportunity, which is of no interest whatsoever to the politicians of other countries. They seem unable to forget domestic conflicts and put themselves in an international framework.

When the name Andrew Peacock comes to mind, I immediately think of Paul Keating calling him the 'sunlamp kid' and saying: 'He's a shiver looking for a spine to run up.' [And I can't help wallowing in Shirley MacLaine referring to his Gucci toothbrush and describing his penis floating in the bathwater … Poor Mr Peacock. He would probably prefer to be remembered some other way.]

Thinking back to those days, often in the background was the shadowy figure of Phillip Adams with his enigmatic smile, rather like the Cheshire Cat.

In 1991, when the Queen came to Australia, Paul Keating, our new Prime Minister, shocked everyone apparently by putting his arm round her back to guide her towards some people she knew. The tabloids were full of it and they called him 'The Lizard of Oz'. A week later I was working for him in Parliament House and he did exactly the same to me — put his arm round my back to lead me into the meeting room. I was indeed honoured to be treated the same way as the Queen!

Visiting Prime Ministers were rather surprised, to put it mildly, to be called by their first name. I remember in particular the President of Argentina who was taken aback by the lack of protocol and formality. He was used to being addressed in a much more deferential manner.

After spending three or four days interpreting for him and Mr Keating, I finally got home at night, tired, and I spoke to my poor long-suffering husband in Spanish without realising it. The more puzzled he looked, the more I increased my volume. Sorry. Professional defect ...

I must confess that the mini-ness of Annita Keating's miniskirt rather took me by surprise, compared with the elegance and sophistication of European prime ministerial wives. Especially when she came into the most private discussions, where even ambassadors were kept waiting outside, and only the two statesmen concerned and their interpreter were allowed in the room. She tiptoed in to re-arrange the flowers, and I longed to take a hairbrush and a few hairpins to her bush of fuzzy hair, to give her a more elegant coiffure.

On the other hand, Paul Keating's dress sense was always impressive — on important occasions one could not help admiring his elegant dark navy double-breasted suits with silver or dark blue ties. He dressed for the part he had to play, which was good psychology and gave him an advantage and in particular an air of authority. But there was nothing hypocritical or devious about him either; he was never afraid to say what he thought. He truly believed in Labour values.

Like Paul Keating, I left school at sixteen; we were both passionate about music, art and good writing, and preferred culture to sports. I admired his direct patronage of the Sydney, and later the Melbourne symphony orchestras, opera, ballet and modern dance. Realising that they had no chance of getting large financial sponsorship like the sports codes, he gave them ministerial grants which made it possible for Frank Moorhouse to write his trilogy, Garth Welch to dance and Geoffrey Tozer to perform on the piano. Like him, I too was a great fan of Graeme Murphy's dance performances and very grateful that thanks to the Prime Minister, the necessary $30,000 was made available to SBS to enable them to record for posterity his 40$^{th}$ birthday dance performance by the Sydney Dance Company.

Also, we both felt that the battle of Gallipoli was a disgraceful waste of human lives and should not be celebrated and, in common with Patrick White, that 'sport had addled the Australian consciousness.'

After a few years I was joined by my daughter who had in the meantime become a member of my profession; her company made it much more fun. Once, when we were working together for Prime Minister Paul Keating, we were told we wouldn't be required for two hours so we dashed off on a shopping spree and spent our earnings in advance. On another occasion we made the most of some unexpected free time by dashing off to the cinema to see *Strictly Ballroom*. Her sense of direction is far superior to mine; she was the brain power behind our short cuts in Parliament House, enabling us to find lifts I would never have known existed. Sometimes we had to interpret at one meeting in one part of the building, say, until ten-thirty and then at another, with different people, starting at ten-thirty in a meeting room in a different part of the building altogether. Working with her we were always on time, wherever we had to be. I shall refrain, however, from saying too much about these short cuts because they probably took us through secret corridors where staff were not allowed.

Like wandering along office corridors on tiptoe at the end of the morning's meeting, and looking through the open office doors where you could see all the public servants eating their lunch from the top drawer of their desk, almost surreptitiously ...

When I first came to Australia, I felt I was coming to an enormous 'English'-speaking continent in Asia, which as such, would soon become a very important Asian country. However, I soon discovered that Australians felt they lived on a small island somewhere off the coast of an enormous, important country called England. Working for Paul Keating was comforting because at last here was someone who understood that we were part of Asia and had an import role to play there. The creation of APEC seemed like a step in the right direction, though I would have preferred some sort of Union of Asian Countries led by Australia to counterbalance the European Union and the United States of America.

Trade discussions with the French Government took place in the prestigious Hyatt Hotel in Canberra. The morning session ended at noon and the Chairman announced: *'You are all invited to lunch in the Griffin Room at twelve-fifteen. Our meeting will resume at one-thirty.'*

A thoughtful member of the organising staff came around to the interpretation booth to tell my colleague and I that we, too, were invited to lunch. We waited until twelve-twenty and then headed for the Griffin Room. We found most people inside, except for the group of French CEOs who were waiting outside in the corridor. One of them told me he had peeped through the doors but no tables had been set up yet. We waited with them for a while and waitresses came round with glasses of orange juice and water but our group refused politely, saying they preferred to wait for the cocktails and wine. After a while, my colleague and I thought we had better investigate so we went through the doors into the Griffin Room. We found side tables against the wall bearing trays with attractive displays of an assortment of open sandwiches: slices of bread with ham and a gherkin, slices of roast beef with a sprig of parsley on top, tuna and egg. We beckoned to the French delegates to come through and suggested they help themselves but they refused politely, saying: 'No thank you, we'll wait for lunch.'

To the average Frenchman, lunch means a chair, a table with a tablecloth, a napkin, a knife and fork, steak, vegetables, maybe some chips and a side salad and a glass of red wine. A synonym for lunch in France is: *'steak frites'*.

When I explained the situation to the French delegates, one of them telephoned the Embassy and soon they were off in two taxis to have lunch there. Needless to say, they were not back on time when the meeting resumed at one-thirty.

\* \* \*

Back in Suva for a meteorological meeting, I once more checked in at the Tradewinds Hotel. This time Rocky was on his own. Julia had decided to go back to New Zealand to pursue her career in photography and had taken the girls with her for the sake of their schooling. Rocky suggested we have dinner in his favourite Chinese restaurant in Suva and then a nightcap at the Yacht Club. When I said I wouldn't have any alcohol because I needed a clear head in the morning for the Seminar, he ordered two 'Claytons', explaining that his liver had been enlarged for some time and had now become a serious matter — he hadn't drunk any alcohol for over a year. I must confess I had noticed he had rather a large bulge and had been trying not to look at it.

We talked over our Claytons and I thought how right Peter had been when he said Rocky was a 'real person' — so different from many 'politically correct' people we knew. His integrity was authentic, with him there were no grey areas. He made no concessions to compromise, sitting on the fence, or anything even slightly shady or doubtful, he was the purest man I had ever met. He was larger-than-life in his own 'Rocky' way. He told me many times how deeply he loved Julia and how much he missed her and the girls.

For the rest of that conference we spent all our evenings together, mostly talking about how much we missed Julia and Peter. Rocky took me into a different world, far removed from international conferences, diplomacy and compromise. On one free day he drove me round the island on a sight-seeing expedition, and on the other he picked me up from the Tradewinds Hotel and we drove along narrow roads through tropical green jungle to the mountains above Suva where a group of his friends were preparing a picnic and barbecue in a clearing. Carol, a friend of Julia's was there with little Jan; there was an English doctor and many other laughing, exuberant people, as well as children of all ages. Then I saw the pools. A whole series of them, one above the other, an amazing sight! The children ran off to the biggest pool to take turns in climbing up, grabbing hold of a rope hanging from a sturdy tree above, and swinging down into the water with a blood-curdling scream! Even little Jan had a try, first with his mother, Carol, and then alone. It was an impressive sight to watch them all; I thoroughly enjoyed the warm, friendly atmosphere.

Suddenly Rocky looked at his watch and announced it was time for him to go to the airport to pick up Echo. When he brought her back, she told us how spoilt and pampered she had been on the plane. Her sticky fingers held a large bag of boiled sweets that the air hostess had given her and a book from her mother to read on the plane.

That evening the whole conference was invited by the Fijian government to a twilight boat trip, followed by cocktails and dinner. I asked if I could take Echo with me. We were picked up from the hotel at 6 o'clock, dressed in our tropical finery — except of course for the Australian delegate in dark suit, white shirt and tie, who I secretly suspected of being a Protestant British subject in disguise.

We clambered out of the bus upon our arrival at the wharf where rum punch was served to us under the palm trees. As we stood there in the twilight, the lights came on in the boats all around us, one at a time, and the stars gradually began to appear in the sky.

We boarded the waiting boat and set off amidst the islands; little by little the lights, first of the Tradewinds and then those of all Suva, faded into the distance. Echo kept asking me to read her book to her; I said I would when we reached the island. As we drew near, we could see a row of ladies in grass skirts, with crowns and bangles of lush green leaves round their ankles and wrists waiting for us, and as the boat pulled into the jetty the music began: guitar, ukulele and voices singing in harmony welcomed us to their island.

We walked along a narrow pathway until we came to a clearing where long tables and benches had been arranged in a circle. More rum punch was served and I found a seat under a palm tree and opened the book. It turned out to be a sex manual for children with many coloured illustrations. I started to read and soon we were surrounded by the boat crew, the hostesses, the cook and an odd assortment of local boys, all heads bent in silence as they listened and concentrated on every detail. After a few chapters I had to stop reading because the food was being served — there were bowls of cooked meat, cassava, roast chicken, salad, cake and all the varieties of Fijian fruit for us to help ourselves. Everyone was kind to Echo, talked to her and gave her the best of everything — she was the star attraction, being the only child there. All she wanted, however, was for me to read more of the book, so in between mouthfuls I continued reading and we were soon surrounded once again by our audience.

When we could eat no more, the dancers reappeared and performed joyful songs and native dances, and I pondered about years gone by, when the missionaries came to convert these happy people to the western way of life and beliefs. How dared they inflict our problems and worries on these happy people? How could they be so arrogant as to think the western way of life was better? It should be the other way around. Complex Europeans with their worries about mortgages, retirement pensions, new cars and keeping up to date with the fashions should learn how to enjoy life from these carefree, happy, relaxed island people.

A dark-skinned man in a red skirt climbed up a tall bending coconut palm in swift, sure movements, and in a few minutes, he was at the top while another man, similarly attired, climbed a lampstand nearby and directed the beam of light on to the coconut palm climber. Once at the top, he threw down an array of coconuts to prove that he had got there; in an agile flash he was down on the ground again. It was as though he had tree-magnets in the soles of his feet and the palms of his hands.

Mosquito Island was well named — I was devoured by them, as was everyone else. The mosquitos were having a party, too. A tall, elegant, genteel English lady started talking to me. She had been living in Fiji for sixteen years. As we watched the Fijian climb the coconut palm, she explained that Fijians have a prehensile big toe, which stands apart and is bigger and longer. 'I am married to a Fijian,' she said 'and my son has a Fijian foot; it's no joke trying to get his feet into European shoes …'

Then two men sat in the grass, and having cut a palm leaf in half, they took one piece each and by deftly cutting, bending and threading, one of them produced a perfect sunhat for Echo and the other a grasshopper, which he gave to me. Thereupon we were grabbed by a passing dancer into the Conga line and whisked away.

After a haunting farewell song in beautiful harmony, we threaded our way back to the waiting boats.

The refreshing breeze on the ride back was pleasant on our faces, under a starry sky; as we approached the shore, the palms stirred and gentle waves lapped at the sand.

Fiji now had coffee. So many coffee plantations had appeared since my last visit that I no longer needed to remember to take supplies for Rocky; soon I discovered their local coffee was quite good.

\* \* \*

I love the atmosphere of the Fijian islands; at peace in my hotel room, with hibiscus flowers decorating the mirrors and bathroom, the view from the windows, with Tanoa on the top of the hill in the distance and all around, lush green slopes and hills with flame trees proclaiming their red presence everywhere I looked, and tall, majestic palm trees. I love the flowers on the food, in people's hair: everywhere. And music. The harmony singing at the slightest provocation. I have always felt completely at home in the tropical Fijian climate, completely at ease with all the relaxed, warm, friendly, smiling Fijian people I have met.

\* \* \*

But it was always good to get home to Canberra to Peter's welcoming arms. When we made love, I felt the secret parts of my body reaching out for him. Later when he went off to work, leaving me luxuriating among the pillows, I felt like a ripe peach or a juicy pear basking in the sunshine on the branch of a tree.

Living with one foot in Switzerland and the other in Australia was beginning to complicate my life unnecessarily. Each time I wanted to wear my red dress in Canberra, the matching shoes and belt were in Geneva. Whenever I needed a book, it was sure to be on the other side of the planet. I finally decided it was time to choose and Australia won. After the carefree open-air lifestyle, the lack of formality, the beautiful birds, flowers, trees and beaches of Australia, Geneva seemed constricted, narrow and cramped. So, as the end of the following six-month stint in Switzerland approached, I took the train to Berne, the capital of Switzerland, and then a taxi to the Australian Embassy to apply for a Permanent Residential Permit.

The burly Australian facing me from the other side of a large desk had a twinkle in his eye.

'G'day,' he greeted me. 'My name's Hugh. Take a pew.'

'I wish to apply for permanent residency …' I began.

'No sweat.' He leant forward. 'Have you ever been in jail. No? Write "No" here.'

He deposited a form in front of me and said:

'When you've filled it in, put your moniker here, attach a picky and I'll give you a bell when it's ready.'

On my way to the door, he added that if I wanted a permit, I would have to do a job that was needed. 'No good saying you're an interpreter or a translator,' he added. 'We don't need linguists; we have plenty of those. Migrants. More than we want. They speak all the languages under the sun. You'd stand a better chance as a road-mender.'

I took careful note of the two accredited medical surgeries in Geneva where I could go for my medical examination, including an eye test. As I left, he called after me: 'I'll give you a tinkle on the blower.'

A few days later the physician congratulated me: 'It's a good job you're not short-sighted. They're not accepting short-sighted people for Australia.'

My application was successful.

I received the distinct impression that English was a superior language and that all others were somehow inferior. In Europe it was the aristocracy who spoke the 'other' languages — French was generally regarded as the language of sophistication — fine wines, expensive clothes and perfumes. The Royal families of Europe spoke French and German — probably had French nannies, — and there had been so many cross-marriages. In Switzerland you had to speak three languages to be a bus driver/conductor or a postman because Switzerland has four official languages, all of equal importance, and English is not one of them. Not so in Australia. If you wanted to get somewhere, you had better stick to English.

My next task was to organise a farewell garden party. I sent out invitations to all my interpreter colleagues who brought food, drink and musical instruments from South America, the Caribbean, Russia, China, France and Spain. About a hundred people said they would come. Peter climbed the trees, installing fairy lights and cables so that we would be able to dance under the stars. A seven-piece New Orleans jazz band would play until 1 am; there would be balloons, a bonfire, a firework display, and the planting of a weeping willow tree. Arian Kirilov said he would be there without fail — it would be his first outing on his new artificial feet, but I hardly dared hope he would be able to come.

Fortunately, the weather was kind: It was a lovely evening. One colleague brought an unexpected visitor who had just arrived from New York — a very courteous gentleman who explained to me that he had started out as a UN interpreter. Later I learnt that he was an Assistant Secretary General from UN New York, in Geneva for a meeting.

The party was in full swing, music playing, couples dancing, glasses clinking when a car drew up and out stepped first Astrid, Arian's girlfriend and driver. Then came Arian on his new feet. The music stopped. The dancers froze. A few moments of incredulous silence and then thunderous clapping as Arian advanced, followed by Astrid, carrying between them the most amazing farewell gift I have ever received: A rolled up carpet! Slowly they moved forward, Arian placing his feet carefully and deliberately one in front of the other. When they reached the centre of the garden, friends sprang up to help as they spread the carpet on the grass and soon people were sitting on it laughing and clinking glasses once more. It was a beautiful, warm summery evening; the warmth and love in people's hearts filled the air and today if I close my eyes, I can still recapture that feeling.

Arian explained: 'I had to have both feet amputated after the mishap in Nairobi — at the ankles — but I had a really good surgeon who removed all the broken bits and the bits that no longer functioned properly.'

'Since the operation it has been an enormous relief to have no more pain. I'm learning to use these protheses, I'm managing quite well — it's only on staircases that I really lack confidence. At home I can walk about without them, which I had never thought possible. I often dream about my feet, sometimes I dream I am running. I can 'feel' them as if they were still there. But I feel better than I have ever been and it's so wonderful to have no more pain.'

As he talked, I could see that he had no sight in one eye …

But Demon Diabetes hadn't finished with Arian. One day, I received a message that he was very ill and wanted to see me. He lived in Ferney-Voltaire in nearby France; I drove there to see him in my beloved turquoise Fiat.

He lay, pale and thin, on white sheets and spoke in a quiet, tired voice. 'The diabetes is winning,' he said with a wry smile. 'I am losing the battle. I am on a hunger-strike.'

His thin, sensitive face looked wan and sad but his eyes shone bright as ever. I remembered his delicate manner, when we were working together, how he coughed politely before speaking and how anxious he always was not to displease.

We talked for a while and he asked me to watch out for Astrid after he had gone. 'Please keep in touch with her, whatever happens,' he asked.

I left, saddened and yet fully understanding how he felt. A hunger strike was the only way out which didn't involve anyone else or risk legal retribution. I decided to keep this possibility in mind for the future for myself, *por si acaso*.

Sadly, however, Arian was not allowed to have his way. He was taken to hospital when he was too weak to protest and fed intravenously.

It was much later, in September 1987, that I received a letter from Astrid telling me Arian had died in hospital in Aberystwyth. He had suddenly fallen ill and stopped eating again. He went from one coma to the next. A few days before his death he came out of the coma and talked peacefully about their life together but later he collapsed without warning and did not recover.

I would never again see his small sensitive, pale face with bright shining eyes, hear his polite cough, or experience his delicate, quiet manner, so anxious not to displease.

Against general opinion, I decided to sell my house in Versoix in order to build one I liked in Australia. With toilet and bathroom windows that really closed and real central heating for the winter.

My son was outraged. How could I sell his 'family home'?

I tried to explain that I had no choice. I needed somewhere to my liking to live in Australia.

I handed in my Swiss *'Permis de Séjour,'* also against general opinion — so many of my colleagues would have given anything to have one — they were extremely hard to obtain.

'What if you don't like Australia?' they asked. 'You won't be able to come back.'

But I knew that going back was not a personality trait of mine.

I closed my Swiss bank account. 'What a mistake!' they all cried knowingly.

This time when we set off for Australia it would be the last time. My official domicile had now switched to the Antipodes.

*　　*　　*

Before leaving Europe, we went on a houseboat tour of Camargue, which is the delta between the Rhône and the Petit-Rhône; a vast area of lagoons, shallow pools where seawater salt is dried in the sun, rice fields and marshes where seabirds breed and wild horses gallop. On the banks as we went by, at the water's edge, we saw fishing, Camargue style: long pivoted, braced fishing poles used to lift nets from the water when the fishermen come back from the café.

We hired a comfortable houseboat in Palavas-les-Flots and travelled along the Rhône past Aigues-Mortes with just the sound of the gentle lapping of the water and the cries of the birds to keep us company: flights of pink flamingos against the blue sky, hundreds of white egrets and later night herons and bustards. On the banks on either side black bulls cavorted and wild horses, mostly white, tossed their manes and galloped past on their slender legs. One never sees overweight horses. Maybe they are wiser than humans.

We passed medieval castles, walled cities and fortresses. We tied up alongside the jetty in Grau-du-Roi — we had arrived just in time to see the jousting. There were two brightly painted and beautifully decorated wooden boats with a wooden construction like a ladder protruding at a 45-degree angle, each with a small platform at the top where the jouster stood, dressed in medieval finery — until he was knocked into the water and ruined his costume.

Saintes-Maries-de-la-Mer, according to ancient tradition, is where the gypsies' pilgrimage takes place in May and October. They say that Marie, the sister of Virgin Mary, and Marie, the mother of James and John, together with their black servant Sara, fled there by boat to escape persecution in Judaea. Relics of the two Maries are preserved in the apse of a twelfth century fortress-church in Saintes-Maries and Sara is the patron saint of the gypsies. They told me that, during the gypsy gatherings, the evenings were devoted to wild music, singing and dancing. What more could anyone wish for? How I wish I could have been there during those festivities ...

Then, as a last farewell to Europe, I rented a small house in Tuscany right in the middle of a little village called Rietine.

My turquoise Fiat dated from 1971; she was getting rather old and creaky and her clutch had begun to slip and made strange groaning noises. This became particularly noticeable during the ten-hour drive from Geneva: shooting along the *autostradi* at top speed (you were not allowed to travel at less than 100 km/h on the autostradi). She was fine and quite at home, but as soon as we got into traffic with a great deal of stopping and starting, she complained. I had done a lot of driving in Italy, mainly in Rome, so driving with one hand on the hooter was no problem, but it was embarrassing when she broke down in the middle of the traffic and it was all the other cars hooting at me. My English upbringing prevented me — even though I was familiar with the vocabulary — from hanging out of the window to return the friendly and quite picturesque abuse that was shouted at me on those occasions (and which frequently offered suggestions as to my mother's profession), generally accompanied by appropriate gestures. I decided to see if I could find a Fiat garage — they were almost all Fiat anyway — once we reached our little village and found our house, to get the clutch and gearbox fixed.

We drove into Valdrano and found a small garage with a large Fiat sign outside. The owner was also the mechanic and the accountant. He greeted me as if we had known one another for years — after all, we were both Fiat lovers. After an inspection and a trial drive he announced his verdict. The gearbox had to be replaced. We asked if he could do it by the weekend when we hoped to leave for Siena and left the car with him after he had driven us home.

At the end of the week, as arranged, he came to take us back to pick up our car. It was late Friday afternoon by the time we got there. 'There she is, as good as new!' he said, proudly indicating my car, freshly washed, polished and sparkling. I tried her while he watched. 'You have rejuvenated her!' I exclaimed.

'When do you leave?'

'First thing tomorrow morning we are off to Siena,' I told him.

'Well,' he replied, 'you had better not pay me now. The banks are closed until Monday. You can't go off on your travels without any money. Take the car and enjoy Siena. Come back and pay me on your way home.'

He was insistent so we left on a cloud of euphoria — I had been warned so often that one had to watch one's handbag in Italy, yet here was a hardworking Italian refusing to be paid out of generosity and thoughtfulness.

It was a pleasure to go back to see him on the way home and settle our account.

When we reached Rietine, the bent old lady dressed entirely in black who gave us the key told us with a friendly, toothless smile, that the village was so small there were no shops so we would have to go into the next village for supplies; it was slightly bigger and had two shops and a café.

Our house was old and made of stone. A few stone

steps led up to a balcony surrounded by a wrought iron balustrade covered with flowering creepers and sweet-smelling rambling roses. We unlocked the heavy, blue, wooden front door and stepped inside onto the cool stone floor, out of the heat.

The ceiling was high, there were rafters and beams and the stone floors were sloping.

A creaky wooden staircase led upstairs to the bedroom and bathroom. There were open fireplaces in the bedroom and in the main room downstairs where the walls were covered from floor to ceiling with laden bookshelves — we felt we could happily spend a few months there working our way through all the books.

There was no telephone, no radio, but the armchairs and sofa looked comfortable and through an archway we could see a large old-fashioned kitchen.

The village church was right opposite our front door — in fact only about five yards away. On our first Sunday morning we were awoken by the church bells. We had breakfast on the balcony just above our front door and the statue of Holy Mary blessed us with outstretched arms every morning as we sipped our tea! We loved to watch the churchgoers arriving and leaving in their Sunday best, chattering amongst themselves as they went.

Our bathroom window at the back of the house opened on to a small square with a well in the middle. Early every morning groups of head-scarved ladies dressed entirely in black awaited their turn to fill their buckets with water, sitting in groups on the steps. Peter, coming from Australia, found this an amazing sight!

We drove up and down hills covered with olive groves and in between chianti vineyards to the next village and tried various varieties of local *chianti classico*. Soon we had our favourite velvety red which we enjoyed on our balcony with fresh crusty village bread and local cheese, while the village people around us went about their business. A little girl was crying and an elderly grandmother in black tried to comfort her, two small boys terrified everyone by shooting about on bicycles ringing their bells and demonstrating all the tricks they could perform on one wheel, while a goat wandered about looking rather perplexed, its dainty neck-bell ringing as it moved. On the far side of the square, a group of elderly villagers sat dozing on a low brick wall, enjoying the warm sun, while a grey-haired woman with her hair in a bun hung out washing from an upstairs window on a clothesline stretching across the street. On all sides we were greeted with *'Buongiorno, signora,' 'buongiorno, signor'* accompanied by friendly smiles as we walked round the narrow cobblestoned streets.

On our way back to Australia we decided to stop for a fortnight in Sri Lanka where Peter's daughter, Julie, had died some years before. I felt he had never really had an opportunity to say goodbye to her; he needed to see the hospital in Colombo where she had died and visit the place where the local minister had planted a yellow frangipani tree in her memory because she had had a yellow ribbon in her beautiful long dark hair when she died.

When we got there, we took a rickshaw first to the hospital, which was a depressing place: overcrowded, with beds all along the corridors, queues everywhere and no air conditioning in spite of the intense heat. Then our rickshaw took us to St. Andrew's Church which, in comparison, we found cool and peaceful: a welcome sanctuary from the great heat, noise and dust outside. Behind the church was Rev. Andrew Baillie's residence but no one was home. I sat in the shade on the grassy slope while Peter walked about, looking at everything. Suddenly a car drove up and out stepped the minister with his sister and their cocker spaniel, Sandy, who limped except when running. When Peter explained why we had come, they were kind and welcoming; they well remembered 'the girl called Julie' with the yellow ribbon in her dark hair. It was now six years since she had died. They had visited her in hospital three times, the last visit at seven in the evening just before she died. Her friend David had collected all her possessions. She had been in a coma for a while — David hadn't understood the seriousness of the situation. Neither had she. She had fallen ill in Kandy and when her condition worsened, she had been advised to come to the hospital in Horton Place, Colombo.

The Reverend's sister, Martha, added that Julie had not been afraid, she had rather been disdainful of death — in fact she had had an elusive half smile which seemed to say: 'Death, you do not frighten me.' Her skin was not yellowish as one might have expected; she died of a collapse of the kidneys, a 'fulminating hepatitis'.

Martha also explained that there would soon be a plaque at the foot of the tree saying: 'In memory of a girl called Julie'.

We went to the Oberoi Hotel for dinner and talked it over, sitting hand in hand, listening to a string quartet playing light classical music and sipping a 'Tropical Itch'. As it was in Kandy that Julie had fallen ill, we decided to go there the following day.

Among the interesting things I learnt was that 'Sri' means 'Lord' or 'Sir,' so it is a title. 'Lanka' means 'island' so 'Sri Lanka' means 'Lord Island' or 'Special Island'. It was certainly that. The old name 'Ceylon' was from the Dutch: 'Zealand'.

Apart from the countless wonderful temples we visited and the impressive enormous one in Kandy — gongs, prayer wheels, oriental music wafting — we saw many curious little houses made of plaited palm leaves hanging between two palm trees by ropes at each end. At first, I thought they were roofed hammocks for children to sleep in, or a birdcage, but in fact they were cages for hens and chicks to protect them at night from the mongoose. In the morning the door at the top of the ladder would be opened to allow them freedom to wander.

Peter was sad yet pleased to have followed the tracks of his beloved daughter, Julie, and to have seen where she had spent the last weeks of her life before she died. Sadly, we drove to the airport and caught our plane to Australia to start a new part of our lives.

Some months later, Cassie asked if she could come to Australia to live with us and study Russian and Philosophy at ANU. I went back to Geneva for a month and we travelled back together. The immigration officer handed me a pink form.

'Sign here, fill in your daughter's details and you'll get an allowance of $18 a fortnight for her,' he explained. I was too amazed and overwhelmed to remember the details. Without asking for anything, without having contributed anything to Australia, I was to be given $18 out of the blue by this generous country, just because I had chosen to come here to live with my daughter!

She had her precious guitar with her. The customs official looked at it doubtfully and asked if she would play something. Not because he loved guitar music, but just to make sure it wasn't full of drugs. She sat on the bench in the middle of the airport hustle and bustle and played the *Alhambra* by Albeniz. Everything stopped. It was a magical moment.

Agnes, a colleague from Switzerland, and I were among the least eccentric of our colleagues. Working under such high pressure often has strange effects on the personality of interpreters. The fact that we drank countless cups of strong black coffee (ristretto) during the day to keep our brains alert, may have something to do with it. One of the top prima donnas, very much in demand, she refused to turn her microphone on when we came back from lunch unless her pencils had been sharpened during the lunch break. She was the one who was furious when, as Chief Interpreter, I telephoned her one morning to let her know that her meeting had been cancelled. 'You're in luck. Your meeting has been cancelled. You can stay in bed,' I announced. Instead, she shouted back at me angrily: 'So why phone and wake me up then, if I can stay in bed? Now I shall have to try and go back to sleep.' I tried in vain to understand her reasoning.

Some colleagues were so stressed that, even though they were working in another booth, I could feel their tension through the cabin wall, even behind my back.

We have to speak as fast as the speaker in order to get to the end of the sentence at the same time, or we might miss something. The chairman might give the floor to someone different in quick succession and we might miss some vital information. In order to gain speed, we learn, after a year or two on the job, to enter the thought process of the speaker, so we know about halfway through, how a sentence will end. This becomes a habit and our friends and families frequently complain that we 'never let them finish'. Simultaneous interpreting is not just a matter of language skill; one also has to be a very quick thinker.

But, to get back to Agnes: she was coming to Australia on her way to a conference somewhere or other and we arranged to have lunch together. We hadn't seen one another for a number of years; there was a mountain of news of colleagues and delegates to catch up on … How could we possibly get it all said in one lunchtime?

'We need at least twenty-four hours' non-stop talking,' I said.

I cannot think of her reply without bursting out laughing. Perhaps it is funny only to simultaneous interpreters. Her brilliant answer was:

'The only way is for us to talk simultaneously.'

Picture two interpreters in a restaurant holding a simultaneous conversation as fast as they can go. With that image I must leave you. I have to rush off to pack. I am off to Tahiti tomorrow for a cardiology conference.

\* \* \*

Sitting at café terraces in Madrid, Geneva or Paris with colleagues, we sometimes commented on men's bottoms as they walked past. Some were trim, muscular and taut in tight-fitting trousers like those worn by Spanish dancers or my handsome gasman in Melbourne. But, at that time, most Australian men I met wore ill-fitting trousers that were so baggy you had no idea what sort of bottom they had. The crotch of most of my husband's friends' and work colleagues' trousers was roughly level with their knees. I came to the conclusion that in Australia in 1980 men lacked self-esteem and were over-shy about displaying their attributes. Often a man's bottom was his best feature. Thank heavens for the invention of blue jeans!

In those days, in the 1970s, it seemed that Australian women's power resided in their frailty. They sat at home pulling strings, deciding what everyone in the family should eat, wear and do, the men cherishing them because they were poor frail things who couldn't even find the strength to carry their own handbags: I noticed so many of my husband's work colleagues carried their wives' handbags when they were out together. Fortunately, everything has changed enormously since then.

I also noticed the feeling of power women had when serving family meals. Instead of the European way of putting the dishes of food in the centre of the table so that each person could take what they liked, the woman of the house decided what each person should have and how much they should eat; it seemed it was the duty of each member of the family to finish what had been put on his/her plate.


It was a shock to find the Tradewinds Hotel closed during one of my conference visits to Suva — apparently because of rising damp. It had become rather dilapidated and the owners, who had now become friends, had warned me during a previous visit that this might happen because the whole building was gradually sinking into the sea — like Venice — and a lot of work and money would apparently be required to bring it back to health standards. It was a relief though to find *Quinquereme* was still there. I left a message for Rocky to say that I was staying at the Travelodge but had a free weekend in the middle of the conference and hoped to see him. I received a reply that he would pick me up at the Travelodge Sunday morning at 11 o'clock.

I waited inside the glass doors of the hotel, and at about five minutes past, an old rather dirty car drew up and I could see Rocky's fuzzy halo of hair through the window. I opened the back car-door and jumped in.

'Thanks,' I said. 'And how are you keeping?'

'We're all right,' he mumbled. 'And you?'

He obviously wasn't in a chatty mood, I thought as I watched the scenery shooting past at high speed. He was driving unusually fast.

After a few minutes' silence, I asked: 'Who do all these smelly sneakers belong to?' The bottom of the car was full of muddy shoes. It was hard to find a spot to put my feet.

He turned around to look at them and I realised in a flash the driver wasn't Rocky. It was an unknown man with a similar fuzzy halo of hair.

'Who are you?' I asked in a panic as we shot through the streets.

'And who are you?' he asked in return.

'I'm so sorry, I got in the wrong car.' I mumbled. Actually, there was a niggling panic in the back of my mind. Supposing this man refused to take me back? Or just dropped me there in the street — I had no idea where I was and we had been driving very fast.

'Would you mind taking me back to the hotel?'

Fortunately. it was a genuine mistake on both sides, and all was well in the end.

'Why didn't you say anything when I got in your car?'

'You seemed to know what you were doing, where you were going, I thought you must be the person I was supposed to pick up.'

Back in the hotel entrance, five minutes later the real Rocky arrived and this time I jumped into the right car.

He seemed lonely and needed to talk. He was extremely thin, obviously not looking after himself very well. His face looked drawn, almost haggard. He had an enormous bulge — at first I thought it was the traditional antipodean 'beer belly' but as he talked I noticed that it was a different shape — in fact it looked more like a pregnancy. At some point in our conversation he noticed my glance and said: 'It's my enlarged liver.'

We spent our evenings together mostly in the Yacht Club or in a nearby Chinese restaurant and I gathered he was still on his own, very sad and lonely.

After that it was a year or two before I had another conference in Fiji, and then I had two meteorological meetings back-to-back, both in Nadi — the weather station there is very important to the region.

There were three French-speakers requiring interpretation and since we were all staying at the same hotel, we soon became a close-knit group, meeting in the dining room for breakfast, lunch and dinner; discussing all manner of things frankly and passionately, as sometimes happens on a conference far away from home, and all one's day-to-day concerns.

We were free on Saturday and decided to hire a minibus to take us to Suva where, after a look around the town, we would have lunch. I found out from the hotel reception desk that the Tradewinds had now been renovated and was open for business again, so we agreed that's where we would go.

We were a happy, talkative group all engaged in meaningful discussion and it was a bright sunny day. I remember we drove past a café with the picturesque name of 'The New Car Shine Café'.

When we arrived at the Tradewinds I asked if we could have my favourite table right at the end of the jetty with the ocean on three sides. It was a joyful occasion, we ordered French wine — a real luxury — and chose our favourite items from the menu; everyone was merry, but I had a strange foreboding feeling I could not understand.

Until I looked around us. The jetty was just wide enough for our table; surrounding us, floating on the water, were flowers. Pink, blue, yellow, mauve, deep-red garlands, crowns and bouquets, individual flowers of all colours floated round and past us ... And continued travelling gently, rippling along the shore towards town. It was an enchanting sight — amazing and unforgettable. At first I felt elated by it and then, gradually, understanding began to pierce through the joy — the elation dissipated and was replaced by sadness and tears.

We were not far from the wharf; I could see people on the deck of *Quinquereme* and groups standing talking along the walkway. Rocky had been buried at sea from *Quinquereme* that morning, to the sound of Colin's bagpipes. We were surrounded by his flowers.

I learnt later that he had lain in state at the Yacht Club because that's where he had spent most of his evenings. Then his coffin had been taken out to sea in *Quinquereme* and flowers had been spread all over the water. All the other boats from the Tradewinds and from town had joined in; they too had put flowers on the water. A commemorative plaque was being placed on Rocky's favourite bar stool at the Yacht Club — Marigold's idea. When Marigold finished her International Baccalaureate in Wellington she planned to return to live in Suva.

It was in December 1981, that Peter and I finally wed. I wanted an alfresco Renoir style wedding à la *Moulin de la Galette* and found two beautiful antique *écru* lace dresses dating from 1905 for Cassie, my bridesmaid, and myself — one in Chelsea, London and the other in Paris. We decreed that all our guests had to be dressed in 1905 style. Peter's son was best man and both he and the groom looked very dashing in their pale grey silk top hats. The ceremony took place in the shade of the eucalypts by the lake in the grounds of University House, Canberra; the day before we had chosen the three gumtrees we wanted to be married under and tied pink ribbons round their trunks.

On the big day, my bridesmaids, flower girls, ring boy and I were driven to the ceremony in an open carriage drawn by a white horse. Peggy Crosskey, in a slinky black dress and large-brimmed white beflowered hat, had set up her harpsichord under one of the chosen gumtrees.

After the ceremony we all sat round large trestle tables decorated with white flowers and balloons to eat and drink; as soon as the marriage certificate was signed, a hundred or so balloons were released. As they rose into the air people gasped — it was a breathtaking sight and suddenly I felt my life had changed once again. Now I was married to an Australian. My life was about to take a new turn. Soon I would have yet another passport to add to my collection.

The jazz band started playing and everyone danced. In 1981, Canberra was quite a serious place and our wedding photos with the balloon release hit the front page of the *Canberra Times*.

We went back to our little house in Page, but since we were planning to leave early the following morning by car to Mildura where we would be boarding a paddle-steamer for two weeks, I had already emptied and cleaned the fridge and the cupboards were bare. No milk. No bread. All we had was wedding cake and a few bottles of champagne for supper and breakfast the next morning, but we survived quite happily.

On board the paddle-steamer *Wanera* everything seemed to be in slow motion; there was little to occupy our waking hours but eating, drinking and watching the water turn different shades of green.

\* \* \*

I think I fell in love with Australia, the country, the first time I saw the beautiful trees, the amazing flowers of all colours and shapes, and the birds. The kangaroos and the wombats, the koalas and the bandicoots, all the marsupials. As for the Australian people, it was in Darwin that I fell in love with them. But first I had better explain the background:

I object to the fact that a woman is expected to change her name every time she changes husbands. It is as though we become our husband's property, which is quite unfair. I hadn't changed who I was when I remarried so why should I change my name? But I had to change it in my passport, my driving licence, my bank account and all my official papers. Why shouldn't it be the husband who changes his name to that of his wife? Everything is so one-sided. Better still, why don't we adopt the Spanish custom of having two surnames, our own plus that of our husband? Or that of your father and your mother so you really know who you are. Or do it the Russian way, with patronyms. Anyway, I decided I would only change my name when I had no choice. As a result, I now have two surnames: a professional one and a married one — which sometimes causes confusion. When the postman knocks at the door and asks me to sign for a delivery, I have to look at the name on the letter or parcel to know which to sign. But I have accepted that as the price of independence.

Around this time, I was asked to be the keynote speaker at a trade conference being held in Darwin. Walking along the streets there after work, I felt very close to Asia. The heat was relaxing, and as in Asia, there were many smells. Pleasant and unpleasant but mostly pleasant because the flowers and plants, like those of Asia, were often fragrant, particularly at sunset. I felt very much at home there and loved the Thursday evening market at Mindil Beach. Being able to speak Spanish with people from Peru, Chile, Uruguay and eat food from their country, buy the most beautiful handmade straw hats, handbags and clothes from the Pacific Islands, kites from Bali and Brazil, exotic plants, sample freshly squeezed tropical fruit juice, listen to music from Hungary and Russia — I felt at peace with the whole planet. Talking to friendly people from Cambodia, Mexico, India, China and Vietnam strengthened this feeling. Instead of the European Union gradually spreading uniformity over all the countries like a cobweb, making all its members conform to the same rules, buy the same things, dress the same way, eat the same food in Madrid, London, Paris as in Amsterdam, Warsaw, Oslo or Milan, here everyone kept their individuality, their native language and their customs and specialities for all to enjoy and appreciate. Multiculturism provided the ideal world.

Australian families came to the beach after work to watch the sunset — instead of going home to shut the door and the windows and watch television from their armchairs. Sitting in groups on picnic rugs were happy families with a lantern on a stick pushed down into the sand, and picnic hampers, bottles of wine, trays of oysters ... the grandparents, the children ... and the most colourful sunset I had ever seen — the sun always seems larger in Darwin than anywhere else in Australia! Everyone watched with bated breath and in sudden silence as the sun approached the sea. Then, when the gigantic ball of orange fire touched the horizon and slowly sank and disappeared, as one they raised their glasses in salute and respect. At that precise moment out of the sky came a sudden amazing array of blue, red, yellow, green and purple parachutes. It was better than the most magnificent firework display: There was grace, spectacle and elegance without the unpleasant explosions in the sky. Like flower blossoms they swayed in the air wherever the breeze took them and then landed gently among us in the sand, and out stepped an assortment of healthy young helmeted people. It was like a five-minute live art exhibition, a burst of colour and life. This country is full of surprises. It was as though some masterful magician had orchestrated that magical moment. In Australia amazing things just seem to happen out of the blue.

The conference organisers had booked my room in a luxury hotel in my professional name.

The conference proceeded. Most days I had lunch in the cafeteria with people I had met but, in the evenings, I was alone in the hotel restaurant because I felt uncomfortable going out to a restaurant on my own.

Wednesday was my birthday and Peter telephoned early — he was off somewhere and the nightwatchman put the call through.

It was a long, dreary day and, in the evening, I decided to be brave and take myself out to dinner for a birthday treat. Feeling homesick for Switzerland, I looked in the Yellow Pages and discovered there was a Swiss restaurant in town. I took a taxi there but, it being mid-week, I was the only client. I tried in vain to strike up a conversation with the waiter while tackling my *rosti*, veal sausage and white wine but I was back in my lonely hotel room by eight with nothing to do but watch television and go to bed.

At 9 o'clock there was a knock at the door. I jumped out of bed, grabbed my dressing-gown and went to see whoever it could be. A chambermaid stood there in uniform, pushing a wheeled table with a white starched tablecloth, a silver bucket of ice with a champagne bottle sticking out of it and a tall glass, a vase of beautiful pink and white flowers and a fruit stand bearing a dazzling array of tropical fruits, all beautifully peeled and cut and arranged in flower shapes.

'Oh no, there's been a mistake,' I stammered. 'I haven't ordered anything.'

She just stood there smiling and handed me a birthday card. Through a mist of tears, I read the birthday wishes, saw the fifteen signatures from the entire staff (except for the nightwatchman who wasn't on duty yet). I was so moved I could hardly speak to say, 'thank you'.

I sat eating the fruit, thinking that they had waited until 9 o'clock to see if anyone telephoned or if there was any mail for me and, when nothing happened, they had decided to take action.

Wonderful, kind people! Just remembering that evening makes me feel warm and fuzzy.

The more I see of the world, the more friendly, generous people I discover.

After a lifetime of simultaneous interpretation in medical research, cardiology, meteorology, telecommunications and agriculture, my brain is full of useless information, rather like a compost heap that has been maturing over the years. Occasionally some of it overflows into my conversation, which must be rather disconcerting and for which I apologise.

The liquid inside young coconuts can be used as a substitute for blood plasma. No piece of paper can be folded in half more than seven times. Donkeys kill more people annually than plane crashes or shark attacks. You burn more calories sleeping than you do watching television. The first product to have a bar code was Wrigley's gum.

The King of Hearts is the only King without a moustache. American Airlines saved US$40,000 in 1987 by eliminating one olive from each salad served in first-class. Venus is the only planet that rotates clockwise. Apples, not caffeine, are more efficient at waking you up in the morning. Most dust particles in your house are made from dead skin. It is possible to lead a cow upstairs, but not downstairs. Dentists recommend that a toothbrush be kept at least six feet away from a toilet to avoid airborne particles resulting from the flush. The average person is about a quarter of an inch taller at night. During a 24-hour period the average human breathes 23,040 times, exercises seven million brain cells and speaks 4,800 words. Human thighbones are as strong as concrete. In a study of 200,000 ostriches over a period of eighty years, no one reported a single case of an ostrich burying its head in the sand. A cough releases an explosive charge of air that moves at speeds of up to 100 kph. On average, people fear spiders more than death. Each year insects eat one third of the world's food crop. A snail can sleep for three years. A hummingbird is the only bird that can fly backwards. Donald Duck comics were banned in Finland because he doesn't wear pants. A full moon always rises at sunset.

Swans are the only birds with penises. Only female ducks can quack. The average human body contains enough potassium to fire a toy cannon and enough iron to make a 7.62 cm nail. Bulletproof vests, fire escapes, laser printers and windshield wipers were all invented by women. The poisonous copperhead snake smells like fresh cut cucumbers. The average human body makes enough carbon for 900 pencils. About 10 per cent of the world's population is left-handed. The first known contraceptive was crocodile dung used by the Egyptians in 2,000 BC. Like fingerprints, everyone's tongue prints are different. If you put a raisin in a glass of champagne it will keep floating to the top and then sink to the bottom. Peanuts are one of the ingredients of dynamite. The electric chair was invented by a dentist. Chocolate stimulates the release of endorphins in the body; endorphins enhance one's mood and block pain. Sydney should have been called 'Albion' but transport was slow and word was received too late, it had already been named Sydney after Lord Sydney. Frogs' hearts continue beating after death — after dissection of the frog they continue beating in the laboratory dish. The average adult human heartbeat is 60–100 bpm, in children it is 70–100 and in the foetus 110–150, whereas in chickens it can reach 400 bpm. The average body temperature in humans is 36.5–37.5, whereas in chickens it is 41–45 degrees Celsius.

Somewhere I learnt that Coca-Cola was originally green and was called '*ke-kou-ke-la*' in Chinese which may mean 'Bite the wax tadpole' or 'female horse stuffed with wax'. After research into the then-40, 000 characters to find a phonetic equivalent, '*ko-kou-ko-le*' was finally chosen, which translates as 'happiness in the mouth'.

When a ball-point pen was first marketed in Mexico, the Spanish translation of its publicity, which should have read 'it won't leak in your pocket and embarrass you,' was thought to mean 'It won't leak in your pocket and make you pregnant' because of the confusion with the Spanish word *'embarazar'* (to impregnate).

A baby food was launched on the African market with the same packaging as in the United States, that is with a picture of a beautiful Caucasian baby on the label. Later the company learnt that in Africa the label generally pictured what is inside the jar for the sake of those who are unable to read.

Somewhere along the way I also picked up information about cockroaches. For example, that they are one of the most widespread and resilient creatures on this planet and that there are over 3,500 species of them. They are practically everywhere around us, hiding in the walls, sewers, and perhaps our cupboards. They are better at sniffing out and eating food than most other insects: the American type has 154 olfactory receptors for smell and 544 gustatory receptors for taste — more than any other insect on the planet! Not only do they like cheese, meat and sugar like the rest of us, but they will also go for things like cardboard, book bindings, human toenails, rotting meat, blood, excrement, and they have been known to eat other dead or crippled cockroaches — all in the name of survival. They can live for nearly a week without their heads. They don't have a highly pressurised network of blood vessels like humans, so they don't bleed out and their necks actually seal off the opening.

They can't regenerate a whole head but do have an impressive set of regenerative superpowers. For up to the first two years of their life, they go through a series of regenerative molts as they mature into adults, during which they can replace lost limbs and over a series of molts, they can regrow antennae and even eyes. Cockroaches can also use our plumbing to climb from sewers up to our bathroom washbasin. And rather a chilling thought: If, one day, there are no humans left on this planet, there may well still be cockroaches.

In my experience, some words are more appropriate in one language than in others. For example, I love the Spanish word for butterfly: *mariposa*. It is so much more appropriate for that delightful, graceful creature than '*papillon*' in French or 'butterfly' in English. The 'mari' part describes its gentle gliding, and the 'posa' part is when it alights on the flower. I would like to create the perfect language where every word is the most descriptive, chosen from all the languages existing in the world.

There are many picturesque expressions that conjure up so much in French, but completely lose their charm when translated into English. For example, if the sky is grey but there is a small, hopeful blue patch, you might say there is enough blue sky to make '*une culotte de gendarme*' — a pair of policeman's trousers. And if someone is beating about the bush without getting to the point but obviously preparing to ask you a favour, you might say '*Je te vois venir avec tes grands pieds*' — 'I can see you coming with your big feet!' If you are still suffering the ill effects of the night before, you might explain that your 'eyes are not yet quite in front of the holes' … '*les yeux pas en face des trous*'. 'A different kettle of fish' is '*une autre paire de manches,*' that is a 'different pair of sleeves,' and a really good wine tastes like '*le petit Jésus en culotte de velours*' — baby Jesus in velvet trousers — my favourite. When the waitress in a low-cut dress bends over to explain the menu to you, you might say '*Il y a du monde au balcon*' — 'there are people on the balcony,' or even 'Ça se bouscule au balcon' — 'the balcony is crowded.'

I will leave you to try these expressions out next time you go to France and see how you get on.

# PART 4
# ULLADULLA

The time had come to choose where we would live when we retired. Australia has 37,000 kms of coastline to choose from. We spent three holidays driving along the coast, investigating all the little side roads and trying the restaurants, between Canberra and Sydney and finally decided upon Ulladulla which was only two and a half hours from Canberra and three and a half from Sydney. We found a spot facing straight out across the ocean — the ocean was at the bottom of our garden.

The digging began in early 1987 and by Christmas that year our house was built; we were able to move in.

We had a little fox terrier called Fifi in those days, and I used to take her for a walk on the beach most mornings. I noticed a young man — probably in his early twenties — lying in the sand, having just come out of the surf, in the shelter of a few trees. He was always there, in the same spot. One morning Fifi went over to give him a sniff; he patted her and we talked.

'This is where I live, here, on the beach. This plastic bag has a change of clothes — 'that's all I need,' he said.

'The government is very kind and gives me money every fortnight — quite enough for food. It's never very cold here.

In winter, if it gets chilly or rains, I just walk into town and have a coffee somewhere warm. What more could I want? I can surf all day, sleep when it gets dark, talk to people on the beach. I have a wonderful life. I want for nothing.'

Every day I stopped for a few minutes to say 'hello,' until one morning he announced that things were about to change. A disaster had befallen. He had fallen in love.

I never saw him again.

\* \* \*

In those early days, I was fascinated by Australian television, so different from the French television I had been used to watching, which was intended to be educational and consisted, apart from news, mainly of documentaries, debates and discussions about music and recently published books, as well as politics. In Australia, I was bowled over by *Prisoner*, *The Midday Show*, *Dallas* and *Dynasty*, where beautiful American heroines went to bed wearing impeccable make-up, with not a hair out of place as they wallowed in sensual glossy satin sheets and pillows. I could see I had been missing out: It was time I tried satin sheets before we were too old. We had reached the 'now or never' stage.

At the top of the hill in Ulladulla was a Grace Brothers store, so off I went to investigate their bed linen department.

The genteel, grey-haired saleslady seemed quite at a loss. She explained in a whispered voice, as if afraid of eavesdroppers, that they didn't stock satin sheets because there was no local demand for them. I couldn't help noticing a 'thank heavens!' sort of expression on her face. People in Ulladulla were obviously too pure for satin sheets.

She said she could order a pair but, she warned, they would be very expensive and would have to be sent from Sydney. Her tone implied that Sydney was the sort of place where people slept on satin sheets, but Ulladulla was definitely not. I began to feel embarrassed but fought against the urge to pretend they were for someone else. Embarrassed by my shamelessness, she looked to the right and left, as she took a catalogue out of a drawer to show me possible colours.

Triumphantly I found exactly the same shade of oyster grey satin sheets and matching pillowslips as I had seen in *Dallas*.

They took a few weeks to arrive. And then, one joyful morning I received the whispered phone message that they awaited me in the store. Jumping joyfully into my car, I drove as fast as I could into town. The saleslady looked over her shoulder from time to time, to make sure we were alone, before handing me the guilty parcel.

When I got home with my shameful parcel, I hid it in the back of the linen-cupboard. I needed time to prepare myself. Some weeks went by before I finally decided 'Tonight would be The Night.' It was a chilly winter's evening and we decided to go to bed early — fortunately, for we didn't get much sleep.

As I snuggled down into bed, my pillow slid onto the

floor. I slid across the bed to pick it up and as I did so, Peter's pillow slid on to the floor the other side. The same thing had happened to him. Three times that night we each had to get out of bed to retrieve our pillows. But that was not the main problem, which was, staying in bed ourselves. The moment either of us moved or tried to turn over, we slid across the bed and landed on the floor. The more we laughed, the more we slid. At one stage when we were both on the floor at the same time we almost decided to stay there. But we are persevering people and it was a cold night.

The following morning, we both looked haggard; I was glad I hadn't told anyone we were trying out our satin sheets that night — they might have thought the worst.

'That's it,' I declared as I stripped the bed and put back the old sheets. I laundered the offending satin ones, put them back in their plastic envelopes and offered them to my friends. 'Have you ever slept in satin sheets?' I asked my neighbour during our local choir rehearsal.

'It's an experience you'll never forget. You really should try while you're young enough to appreciate them.'

With a knowing look, she eagerly accepted the offer and went off home with a smug smile on her face and a big parcel under her arm.

When we met the following week, she handed the parcel back. 'We tried them but no thank you.'

The sheets went the rounds; there was always a willing taker who went home like a cat with a bowl of cream.

Until they finally ended up as a wedding gift for someone's daughter. I can't help smiling to myself as I imagine her wedding night.

* * *

From my windows I see pods of dolphins splashing about in the waves most mornings, and twice a year, whales join in, too, their big black shiny bodies coming up out of the water from time to time, with their distinctive sprays. This morning I saw four humpbacks.

During my absences on conferences, Peter helped the local fishermen with their radar equipment and radio beacons, installing simplified computer systems so they could measure sea temperatures, thus ascertaining where to look for which fish. He hated asking for any payment. As a result, our fridge and freezer were always full of gifts of every type of fish — even the occasional crayfish. I asked him to take me down to the harbour one morning to thank the fishermen. That is where I met Joe, a very easy-going, straight forward, kindly man, who met us with a big smile. Peter thanked him and said the fish had been 'the best he had ever tasted' and Joe said: 'If you need fish, you come to me, if I need electronics, I come to you.'

From that moment on, whenever Peter went down to the harbour, he came back loaded with freshly caught fish. Sometimes he took some canna lily plants from the garden to give the fishermen in exchange, and over the years we watched them flower and prosper among the piles of fish crates on the wharf.

'You have beautiful palm trees in your garden,' Joe said. 'I admire them every time I go down to the beach. Palm trees are the only plants I know.'

'Come round to our place whenever you like,' Peter replied. 'My wife will show you our garden and tell you the names of all the plants.'

It never happened but teaching a fisherman the names of the flowers in our garden was a romantic idea that appealed to me enormously. I liked the fact that Peter lived in the sort of world where such things happened.

\* \* \*

There have been two spring miracles.

In Switzerland, when my children were small, we sometimes took them up to the nearby mountains for a Sunday picnic. In springtime we drove along to the other end of the lake and then up to Les Avants above Montreux and into the forest where the mountainside was white with wild narcissus. Their heady scent was almost intoxicating as we lay down our red and white check tablecloth and installed ourselves in the shade of a pine tree. The children would tumble about, rolling down the mountainside among the flowers, falling over one another and laughing. Once we had finished eating and drinking, we would get our baskets out of the boot of the car — one each, different sizes — and fill them with flowers. In my mind's eye I can see the three children with their arms full of white blooms, my little boy's blond curls bright in the sunshine and the two girls in their first summer dresses of the year. There were hundreds of flowers all around; even though our baskets were full when we left, what we had taken had made no difference.

At home we put vases of wild narcissus in every room of the house. In fact, writing about it now, I can smell that magical fragrance all round me here in the Antipodes …

All my friends respected this Swiss tradition — the scent of wild narcissus meant spring had come at last and the snow and the icy *Bise* were almost over.

All this was more than fifty years ago. Now I live in the Antipodes, I am far from the Swiss mountains. I love the ocean, the crashing waves, the passing dolphins and occasional whales but when I stand, looking at the horizon, I must confess I sometimes miss the three white peaks of the Mont Blanc in the distance. Especially in the late afternoon when they turned pink as the sun began to set …

But the other day we were having lunch in the garden facing the sea when I thought I could see a patch of wild Swiss narcissus in the grass at the bottom of the garden. At first I dismissed the thought — I must be dreaming.

I ate my lunch in a mood of excitement and the moment I had swallowed the last mouthful I called the dog and we went down the slope to investigate. There, incredibly, I found it. Unmistakably, proudly, a patch of beautiful wild narcissus. I stood still for a moment breathing in the fragrance. Reason told me this could not be. The climate here is so different and the altitude too — sea level — I must be hallucinating, transported into the past, into another world. Advancing years were getting the better of my brain. But no, the flowers really were there, standing proudly, almost triumphantly, facing the sea. I bent down and picked a small bunch to take into the house and put in a vase where I could see them, enjoy their fragrance and keep an eye on them to make sure they didn't disappear ...

I still can't believe they were really there. I look forward to next spring to see if they come back.

It was only a few weeks later, again having lunch in the garden, that I saw just a few feet away from the table a single English bluebell. Just one. For a minute I was transported back to my childhood and to Sunday walks in Ruislip Woods or trips to the New Forest. I went to examine it carefully. It really was there and it had healthy green leaves and the bluest of blue flowers.

There is magic in my garden here by the sea in the Antipodes. I believe anything can happen, anything at all ...

\* \* \*

I have pictures in my mind, moving pictures like a living art gallery, but mine have sounds and feelings too. I can conjure them up at will and wander around my gallery enjoying them when I am at peace with the world.

I see a picture of myself as a small child, sitting on a

blanket on the lawn with my mother and my small sister at our house in Ruislip, England. 'If you are good, I'll tell you a story this afternoon,' my mother would promise. This was a special treat; we would excitedly prepare a tray with glasses and a jug of homemade lemonade. My mother had an amazing imagination and could weave an enchanting tale about almost anything — the flowers around us, the bees, the birds, the insects. We didn't want her to stop and kept asking questions, to make the magic moment last as long as possible.

Another picture is of the day I was given the chance to try simultaneous interpretation, out of the blue. In those days, I was a mere translator. Two interpreters had crashed their car into a tram in Geneva on their way back from lunch — it was raining, and the car wheels had somehow got caught in the tram lines. Panic took over the Linguistic Department. It was 2 o'clock and the afternoon meeting at UN was about to begin when the telephone call came through from the hospital. It was impossible to find replacement interpreters at such short notice. I volunteered to try, without really understanding what was involved.

It was a momentous challenge — I had no idea what all the switches and controls were for or how the microphone worked. I still find it hard to believe I was successful. It was an ordinary conference day like any other, until suddenly I found myself in the booth. It was my moment of glory and the turning point of my career.

Another of my mind pictures is of Robert Oppenheimer

and I, sitting in a corner quietly talking, in the hubbub of a cocktail party at a friend's house in Geneva. It must have been more than fifty years ago, yet his pink face and sparkling blue eyes are still as clear to me as if it had happened last week. He was a very gentle, kind man, quietly spoken. Slim, with delicate features — the little hair he still had was snow white. Most of all, I remember his piercing, bright blue eyes and how they sparkled.

Everyone was talking and laughing, trying to hold a glass and a canapé without dropping either, people were pushing past to greet their friends. Light-hearted banter was all around yet, somehow, we both gravitated into a quiet corner and, side by side on a sofa, discussed life after death very seriously. He was very erudite; he seemed to have multifaceted intellectual interests and a profound knowledge of Hinduism. I remember he frequently quoted from the Bhagavad Gita in particular: 'Now I am become Death, the destroyer of worlds.'

Another of the pictures in my mind is of the King of Spain, young, blond and handsome. He had come to United Nations in Geneva for some reason and I was his interpreter. I was in my twenties or early thirties; we chatted a lot and got on very well together.

I remember, too, one evening in Brazzaville when I felt part of a picture. I was standing by the water, watching a group of African villagers washing their clothes at the water's edge. The picture was framed by trees — the most beautiful trees in the world are in Africa — and I was engulfed and enchanted by the green-ness of it all, so many different shades of green — there must have been a thousand different shades. I was spellbound by the clear reflections in the lapping water and above all by the peace, the utter peace of the scene; I felt in perfect harmony with the universe.

So many living pictures in the art gallery in my head!

Peter and I on the beach on the Isle of Wight, feeling young and adventurous although we were both fifty by then, looking up at the row of white and grey-haired old-age pensioners sitting in a double row of old-fashioned wood and canvas deck chairs, along the pavement above. They wore floppy sunhats, concentrating as they poured tea from their thermos flasks and passed metal cups to one another, to avoid spilling the precious contents. Peter made me stand still on the beach while he drew a magic circle round me in the sand, to protect me from evil. I believe it worked.

And then there is another picture on a beach somewhere — perhaps in Ibiza? — when a freak wave wetted our cameras and clothes. I can still see that multi-coloured kite (which he just happened to have in his car), aloft in the deep blue sky above, with my red batik skirt tied to it to dry.

And that magic last afternoon on the *Solent Dove* when we made love as the water lapped the hull peacefully and seagulls flew by, screaming; through the open hatch I could see the swaying mast against the blue, blue sky.

And now here I am, today, strolling along 'my' beach, at the water's edge, my bare feet occasionally bathed by the lapping of a gentle wave. This is 'my' beach because I have tamed it, I know its every detail, even some of its secrets. I am wearing no corsets — the last ones I owned ended up in Swan and Edgar's ladies' room waste bin half a century ago. Not even a bra. And no make-up or nail varnish. There is no lacquer on my hair and high heels are a thing of the past. My life is approaching its end. I have no mink coats or diamond rings. But what I have lived and learnt is a thousand times more precious.

The passing pod of dolphins just a few metres away is almost too much. This must be the happy-ever-after.

*The End*

www.ingramcontent.com/pod-product-compliance
Lightning Source LLC
Chambersburg PA
CBHW021143080526
44588CB00008B/198